The Art of Constructivist Teaching
in the Primary School

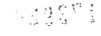

Constructivist Teaching

*a progressive teaching method which works with,
not against, the child's own conceptions*

The Art of Constructivist Teaching in the Primary School

A Guide for Students and Teachers

Nick Selley

David Fulton Publishers
London

David Fulton Publishers Ltd
The Chiswick Centre, 414 Chiswick High Road, London W4 5TF
www.fultonpublishers.co.uk

First published in Great Britain in 1999 by David Fulton Publishers

Note: The rights of Nick J. Selley to be identified as the authors of this work have
been asserted by him in accordance with the Copyright, Designs and Patents Act
1988.

David Fulton Publishers is a division of Granada Learning Limited, part of
Granada plc.

British Library Cataloguing in Publication Data
A catalogue record for this book is available from the British Library.

ISBN 1-85346-572-0

Typeset by Helen Skelton, London

Contents

Preface

This book arose from a growing awareness of our students teachers' need for an easy, informative and *inspiring* book about the constructivist approach. On hearing that label, students tend to react either with, 'Isn't that marvellous – the answer to all my problems', or 'Sounds fine in theory, but I couldn't do it'. Both are wrong. This book may help to get the balance right.

The idea of teaching in such a way as to encourage mutual communication, interpretation and personal development is not new, and has been advocated – but rarely adopted – for the last hundred years. It has been recommended as an approach to language teaching (*see* Barnes 1976) and of course for moral and social education. But it was in the area of science education that the term 'constructivist' first became well known, and many of the books, chapters and articles for novice teachers are in that context (a good place to start, indeed, because of the need to steer teachers well away from the transmission style of teaching science to which most of them may have been subjected at secondary school!).

Since most teachers are not science specialists it seemed a mistake to associate constructivism too closely with science. So I decided to try to present the approach as part of the art of teaching in general, and that is what Part I sets out to do. The discussion is about how children learn, though without neglecting the fact that *what* they learn is also the teacher's concern. I have not tried to conceal the difficulties and obstacles which are likely to be encountered, because knowledge of these (and some strategies to circumvent them) is an essential tool for the newly qualified teacher (NQT). I have also tried to show how the adoption of this approach can enhance both the children's happiness and the teacher's satisfaction.

Part II consists of chapters about specific curriculum subjects which can be read in any order, to suit the needs of the moment. The contents will turn out not to be ready-made lesson plans but, rather, exemplars illustrating the application of the constructvist approach in various contexts. As such they may well be suggestive of strategies and activities suitable for many different topics. Part II is a little more demanding, and considers some of the philosophical foundations for the theory of knowledge construction.

A trial version of this book was made available to Initial Teacher Education students at Kingston in 1997–8; Part I was used in the Education Studies course, while Part II contributed to School Experience preparation. I am grateful to individuals who pointed out obscurities or (apparent) contradictions in the text, and to those who brought up more general queries about the pedagogy or 'theory-about-practice'. I have also been delighted and intrigued by the anecdotal reports from those who researched their children's ideas in the classroom.

It is a pleasure to acknowledge my gratitude to the many primary teachers who have welcomed me into their classrooms and shared with me their enthusiasm for teaching. My colleagues at Kingston University – Ken Robson, Di Hannon, Jane Maloney, Ray Markson and Alison Pickering – have been unstinting with their time and encouragement, and in their support of the ideals of 'theory-as-lived-in-practice'. Jonathan Osborne and Martin Monk at Kings College London; Pam Wadsworth and Barbara Wyvill at the University of North London; and colleagues at Reading have contributed greatly to the development and clarification of my views (though please do not hold them responsible!).

To conclude, I hope this little book will revitalize some practising teachers' faith in the art of teaching; and I suggest that for the NQTs it may provide at least a first look at what the method has to offer – and perhaps some advice on 'How to go Constructivist and Survive'.

Nick Selley
Kingston University
August 1998

Acknowledgements

Thanks are due to Fontana Press for permission to reproduce passages from Tizard and Hughes (1984) in Exercise 3.3; and also to Jeff Duke and Rebecca O'Grady for the attractive drawings in Figures 1 and 4.

Introduction

Primary teachers, and especially primary headteachers, have not had an easy time lately. The last ten years have seen an unprecedented centralisation of control, most conspicuously the imposition of the National Curriculum (NC) and the power to inspect schools for their adherence to it. And now, to ensure that no loophole is left unsealed, there is a compulsory curriculum for the 'training' (sic) of teachers, almost entirely committed to literacy, numeracy, and science. These changes were achieved not, on the whole, by negotiation, persuasion and reflective soul-searching by the practitioners, but by the force of law, accompanied by the 'rhetoric of derision' to undermine the self-confidence which teachers once had in their own professional judgements. That is history, and the manner in which the NC and its assessment were brought in (the panic, the burden of paperwork, the personal distress, the early retirements) is no longer the issue. What matters is how to retain the best and enhance the quality of education in schools (and in teacher education institutions), within the structure now set by the NC.

Actually, now that we have got used to it (and after the Dearing reforms), almost no-one objects to the NC *as such*, especially if we include the non-statutory documents and the non-assessed introductions to the Programmes of Study. The harm, if any, springs from the tests and 'league tables' of school-by-school performance (exacerbated by funding consequences). The two main troubles are 1) the restriction of testing to just *part* of the curriculum, and 2) the nature of the test instruments.

Primary schools play an important part in the young child's life, and the teaching of literacy, numeracy and scientific enquiry must come high on any list of aims; but nearly (or even equally) as important is the ability to think for oneself, to make reasonable decisions, and to feel comfortable with the physical and social environment (including culture, art, nature and personal relations).

Twenty years ago Elliot Eisner, noting the accelerating trend towards the use of SATs in US schools, warned that:

> Testing programs not only describe, they prescribe ... what is not easily tested is frequently neglected [producing a] differential in the kinds of information made available to the public. One of the most effective ways to create an educational crisis is to develop a norm-referenced achievement test, administer it widely, and attach significant social consequences to its results.
>
> (Eisner 1982:15)

The reason for this is that however high the mean rises, there will always be a large number of students who score below average, and who can thus be described (by the ignorant or the malicious) as 'failing'. Few head-teachers or governors can withstand the pressure to 'achieve' in the curriculum areas subject to testing, even at the cost of neglecting other essential aspects.

The other worry is the style of the tests. If, as seems to be settled now, they are itemized short-answer tests, the perception will be that what will be rewarded is the rapid recall of fragmented information or specific skills. Teachers may resort to making their pupils practise past test papers; and question-spotting will, in the staff room, come to rival the National Lottery as a pastime.

More pernicious still is the possibility that school experience will teach the pupils that achievement in life is success in tests. Children will come to enjoy, above all other intellectual reward, the successful completion of a page of exercises which require no imagination, synthesis of ideas, or even serious engagement. Children of five or six will rush through their 'Readers', not for any pleasure in the story, but in order to move a step up the Reading Ladder. They will engage in investigations with the intention of 'finding out', as quickly as possible, exactly what it is that their teacher is giving the marks for.

It is my wish, in this book, to help teachers and apprentice teachers to resist such a slide towards the mediocre, and to harness the power of the NC for a nobler purpose, that of providing a full and ultimately worthwhile education. Dedicated teachers, who know their pupils as individual people, will be able to select suitable educational objectives from the NC, and then work collaboratively with the children so that the outcome is not only testable knowledge but mental growth, stability and power. 'Knowledge is power'? Maybe so, but only if it can be used in thinking (argument, explanation, prediction) in contexts beyond that in which it was learnt. Some SATs items do require this fluency, and cannot be answered by recall alone. The test compilers are professionals in the field, and are fully aware of the issue of validity – so my second worry, the cramping of the teacher's style, may eventually be resolved, with goodwill and a little extra funding (to pay for the marking of those more sophisticated SATs).

Some teachers are sad but resigned: 'Teaching Year 6 just isn't fun any more. They're bursting with ideas at that age, but we can't afford the time'. Others are in black despair: 'Tests and assessment and recording! Whatever happened to the free spirit of primary education that I was trained for?'

I can only say that the destruction of primary education was not the intended outcome of the 'accountability' movement, and if it is happening, it is an unwanted side effect. It can be avoided by intelligent action by government (through improving the assessment methods) and by teachers (through refusing the temptation or coercion to 'teach to the test'). A moratorium on the publishing of SATs results would help, too.

So, what choice do class teachers have? It is true that the NC is a legally binding document, and that teachers have a duty to administer the SATs. But they are, thankfully, free to use their professional judgement as to the appropriate methodology for teaching. They may, but are not obliged to, use pre-published systematic (so-called 'teacher-proof') schemes; and they may incorporate repetitive exercises of a closed nature. Or they may organise groups to research a topic and then discuss some awkward questions. But my own preference, as a method which has the best chance of resulting in permanent, meaningful learning is the constructivist approach, which is quite well known (sometimes under other names), but which deserves to be more widely used.

Part I
General Theory

Each of us can only learn by making sense of what happens to us through actively constructing a world for ourselves.

Douglas Barnes (Oracy Project)

CHAPTER 1

Constructivist Learning

The constructivist approach to primary education is not a new type of curriculum. It is an approach, or a teaching method. It can be used to augment, partially to replace, and usually to improve existing classroom methods.

For student teachers especially, I must stress that a constructivist approach is compatible with any curriculum, as required by any school; but of course the extent to which it can be utilised will vary according to the ethos of the school. The more the children's own learning (rather than the content of the curriculum) is given priority, the more successful will be the adoption of constructivist teaching.

To start with, let's try to give a rough idea of what constructivism is. At one level, it is a theory of learning which holds that every learner *constructs* his or her ideas, as opposed to receiving them, complete and correct, from a teacher or authority source. This construction is an internal, personal and often unconscious process. It consists largely of reinterpreting bits and pieces of knowledge – some obtained from first-hand personal experience, but some from communication with other people – to build a satisfactory and coherent picture of the world. This 'world' may include areas which are physical, social, emotional or philosophical.

This view of learning is already well known, in the simple sense that (in the words of Douglas Barnes 1992:123), 'each of us can only learn by making sense of what happens to us through actively constructing a world for ourselves'. The crucial question is: what is an appropriate role for the teacher in helping a pupil to construct a successful model of the world? This will be examined in Chapter 3.

An immediate, although negative, significance of constructivism for the teacher is that it suggests that traditional 'transmission' teaching, typified by the lecture, the sermon, and the textbook, may be a very inefficient method. Much of what is 'taught' (i.e. sent out towards the student) will be misconstrued, garbled, or ignored. Most of us can recall the experience of

3

failing to learn what someone has been teaching. Sometimes it has gone on, either tediously or frustratingly, for years.

A better way would be for the teacher to find out, or make an estimate of, what the student already knows about the subject, and start from there. This would avoid the boring repetition of what was already thoroughly known; and the futility of teaching information that was incomprehensible. Ideally, the teacher should help the learners to develop their existing ideas and concepts. This will involve working *with* (rather than sidelining) these ideas: examining their applicability and effectiveness, and suggesting small, manageable improvements. To get to this position, the teacher needs to know of some techniques for drawing out or eliciting pupils' ideas. This will be discussed in Chapter 2.

Then, after elicitation and formative assessment leading to a rough picture of the various pupils' ideas, the teacher will need to use appropriate pedagogical techniques. The aim is to encourage pupils to expand and refine their conceptual powers (I say 'encourage' rather than 'teach' here, because personal growth cannot be forced. 'You can lead a horse to water, but you can't make him drink').

Compared to the transmission mode, the constructivist approach is child-centred. But this is not to suggest that the teacher just sits on the sidelines while the child 'grows'. On the contrary, constructivist teaching requires the teacher to take a very active role, and one which calls upon expertise,

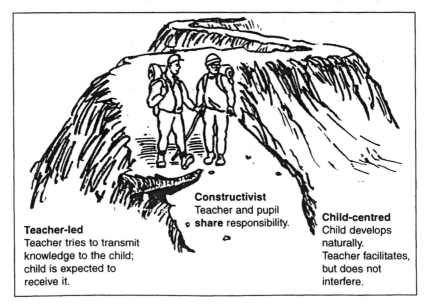

Teacher-led
Teacher tries to transmit knowledge to the child; child is expected to receive it.

Constructivist
Teacher and pupil share responsibility.

Child-centred
Child develops naturally. Teacher facilitates, but does not interfere.

Figure 1 The constructivist approach is a middle way
– and a higher way.

knowledge, and professionalism. It is a middle way, but also a higher way than either the didactic transmission mode or unguided discovery. I have attempted to represent this by analogy with a way along a ridge (Figure 1). The associated danger of falling off, one side or the other, is a known feature of such paths.

The constructivist approach is not appropriate to all school learning. Some knowledge, if it is of the factual kind, or defined by convention, may need to be transmitted directly; for in such cases, creativity or personal imagination are not required, and any alteration would not be beneficial. Examples might include learning the alphabet, spelling, the rules of punctuation; the symbols used in arithmetic; the points of the compass; and the national anthem.

However, much rote learning is of vocabulary – words which refer to particular ideas. The names are easy to learn once the child knows what they refer to, but an unrewarding chore otherwise. For example, it would be misguided to try to teach the names North, North-east, East etc. to a young child who had no sense of direction, and was still unsure even of right and left. So it might be wise to use constructivist methods to determine whether the children were ready for learning certain things, even if these seemed merely factual.

YOU MUST DISTINGUISH	FROM
prescribed (closed) knowledge:	**personal (open) knowledge:**
of facts and conventions;	understanding, explanation,
or of methods and skills;	prediction;
or algorithms and mnemonics.	application, choice of methods;
	judgement of quality and value of
	the knowledge.

Figure 2 A classification of knowledge. Transmission methods may be used for teaching prescribed knowledge, but not for personal knowledge.

It might be useful now to state what constructivist learning is *not*. It is not just any pedagogy which involves the pupils in activity and participation, for sometimes this activity does not contribute to the construction of knowledge. Examples of non-constructivist 'active learning' include: (a) science practical work based on following instructions; (b) 'gap-filling' exercises, with the missing words listed at the base of the worksheet; (c) pictures to label; and (d) information to extract from a text. I would exclude all these because, despite the activity, the learner is being allowed no part in deciding what it all *means*. The teacher keeps control of that, and uses ticks and crosses to enforce compliance.

To sum up, the constructivist approach is not:
- just the provision of tasks for pupils to engage in;
- a 'project' in which predetermined information has to be found (e.g. in books, CD-Roms, or museums);
- a practical activity conducted according to a predetermined method, even if this is called an 'investigation' (unless, that is, the objective is for the children to discuss and interpret, entirely freely, the results which they obtain);
- the kind of lesson which leads children to an achievement which is exactly what the teacher expected.

But the constructivist approach is an ideology that places emphasis on the meaning and significance of what the child learns, and the child's active participation in constructing this meaning.

It is important for every teacher, with any sympathies for constructivism, to be very clear as to its theoretical and evidential base, not only because this is likely to enhance the effectiveness of that teaching, but also because of the likelihood that the method will have to be defended against misconceived attack (see also Chapter 5). As Andrew Davis put it (Davis & Pettitt 1994:3), 'Views of teaching and learning held by politically influential groups are in stark contrast to constructivism, and in such a climate it is especially important to be able to support practice with a coherent and readily justifiable theoretical position.'

CHAPTER 2

Children's Alternative Ideas

I shall first consider ways by which a teacher can get to know what any individual child's presuppositions are, about some given topic. Clearly the most obvious way, though not the most commonly practised, is actually to *listen* to what the child has to say about it. This is most effective after the child has had some opportunity to think about the subject: possibly through a question or task, tackled without haste. The elicitation of ideas will probably need either a quiet moment alone or a small group discussion. It is well worth the trouble to tape-record these conversations, to aid the memory.

The problem of recording the ideas of the whole class at once, with children who are not fluent at writing, is often solved through drawing. Most children are willing to make an attempt to express their thoughts in a drawing, and the teacher can then use this as a starting point for further probing, by private conversation in the classroom. The extra information elicited in this way can easily be written on the page, either alongside the drawing, or as labelling for parts of it.

A similar device, to help children to capture their thoughts on paper, is the 'concept map'. Firstly you should produce a set of words related to the topic, either chosen in advance, or generated through a 'brainstorming' session. The pupils start with one significant word, and write it in the middle of a blank sheet of paper. They then choose a second word, which they can relate meaningfully to the first, and write it nearby. Both words are placed in boxes, which are joined by a line. Older children may then write, along the line, what the relationship is. (Younger ones will communicate this orally.) Then further words are added to the 'map', until all meaningful links have been shown. As with the drawings, it is generally necessary to ask the child for a verbal expansion of the ideas captured on the map.

Every child's ideas will differ, to some extent, from those of any other child. However, it is found that there are often sufficient resemblances to make it worthwhile to select some of the more typical ideas. A teacher,

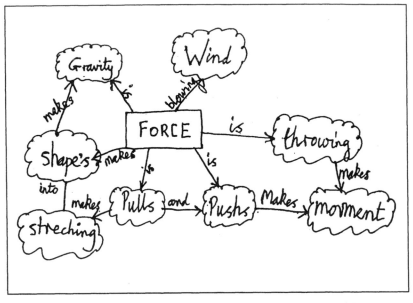

Figure 3 A concept map produced by a Year 6 child,
from Comber and Johnson (1995).

having elicited responses from her class, will naturally spot the most common contributions, and may also make a rough count of those which are approaching, or still far from, the approved version.

Published research

The teacher will be severely limited by time (both for collecting full and detailed accounts, and for the analysis), and by the small size of the population being studied. However, educational researchers have been engaged in this kind of activity for many years, and have collected a wealth of data, especially in the science area. Their methodology has usually been one of the following, and I shall briefly consider the advantages of each:

1. Written tests, usually requiring short answers, but sometimes including completion of drawings or diagrams. The advantage is that these can be administered to large numbers of children, in pursuit of statistical reliability – that is, assurance that the results are typical for the population being tested. The disadvantage is that the children's responses are often ambiguous or unclear, and there is nothing that can be done to sort this out. There is no way of distinguishing between a child who genuinely holds an unusual view, and one who merely misread the question.

2. Requests to children to make drawings (sometimes annotated by the child or, for slow writers, by dictation to an adult) showing their ideas on a given question. This method requires more time, because every child must be visited by an adult before the task can be considered finished, to check on what the child has interpreted the task to be, and what the drawing represents. The advantage of this method is that it is open-ended, and often elicits individual ideas which the teacher/researcher had not imagined, and would not have been asked about in a pre-set test.

3. Semi-structured individual interview. This last method usually takes place after familiarization activities, and the questions are focused on real objects or drawings showing situations which require explanations. The interviewer has a prepared set of questions, but is ready to follow up any unexpected or novel ideas which emerge in the child's answers. The conversations are recorded, and considerable time and labour will be required to transcribe and analyse these (see Selley (1995 and 1996) for examples). The advantage is that if the interviewer can gain the child's trust, then genuinely held beliefs can be uncovered. It is also possible to distinguish stable, firmly-held ideas from guesses or hastily produced responses. All this useful revelation will come about only if the child is sure that the occasion is not like a test, and that her/his own views will be accepted and respected. In this regard the interview resembles a conversation.

The originator of this area of study was Jean Piaget, who was particularly interested in the development of rationality in the child. The wide range of topics which he studied included growth, movement, the material world, chance and probability, proportion and morality. After some decades of neglect, interest in young people's construction of reality was revived by Roger Osborne in New Zealand, particularly for physics. Among the foremost of contemporary British researchers we may note Rosalind Driver (who died in 1998) and Martin Hughes.

While collecting examples of alternative conceptions is of great interest in its own right, some scholars have attempted to go further, using a kind of study known as phenomenography (see Selley 1996: 81). This involves a more refined form of classification and analysis of the concepts held by members of the chosen population. Firstly, the ideas about a given phenomenon are classified into a small number of 'models', these being a concise form of the ideas or beliefs which people use to explain the phenomenon under review. Then a hypothetical proposal is made as to the developmental relationship between these models. Often there will be reason to propose that there is a hierarchical order, such that most pupils move through the various alternatives in much the same order.

Clearly, if this phenomenographical information could be confirmed and then published, teachers would find it of great value when planning their teaching, either to a whole class or when providing differentiated instruction (or interventions) for individuals. The hope is that teachers, by assessing the child's present level of understanding of a topic, will be able to predict in what direction the next advance is most likely to come; and so, what shift of ideas is both desirable and possible.

One of the most influential of such sources in the UK was the Primary SPACE Project[1]. The Nuffield Primary Science resources include teachers' guides for around eight individual topics, with samples of children's work to exemplify their alternative conceptions[2].

Exercise 2.1 Eliciting knowledge

Work in pairs: one will be referred to as Student A, the other B. Each student will, in turn, elicit the other's knowledge about some concept.

Before starting the interviews, you should each choose a subject of which you have expert knowledge (e.g. your Subject Study); and then select one topic which is, to an extent, known to the general public, but is not especially well known to your partner. Check that your partner, Student B, has no objection to your selection.

Student A, having chosen Topic A, must devise a situation (conveyed in writing and/or drawing) which will serve as a starting-point for probing Student B's ideas on Topic A; and vice-versa.

Student A now interviews Student B for a set time (e.g. ten minutes), and keeps notes. No teaching is to be attempted at this stage. After a short break, and time to complete the notes, the roles are reversed.

Finally, you should each write a brief account of your interviewee's conceptual model, and highlight any ways in which this differs from that of yourself, the interviewer. These reports will be needed again, for Exercise 3.1.

As a group activity: work in groups of four, as double pairs. While one pair proceeds with its interview (as above), the other two act as an audience, not joining in until the analysis stage after the interview has ended.

Progression

Progression in learning has attracted attention for some time. Sometimes educationists have made assumptions as to what sequence or hierarchy of

---

1 Primary SPACE (Science Processes And Concept Exploration) Research Reports (1990-94); various authors including Terry Russell and Dorothy Watt; Jonathan Osborne, Pamela Wadsworth.
2 Nuffield Primary Science (1995) *Teachers' Handbook* (and the Teachers' Guides for individual topics at KS1 and 2), Collins Educational.

knowledge the learner ought to follow; but if these assumptions are based on a traditional syllabus, or on some logical order of knowledge items, they may be completely misleading. There may be unsuspected barriers to progress, which only careful research will reveal. There may be social and language factors, which control whether the learner will regard the offer of new knowledge as worth making an effort for, or as an unwanted burden. These issues of intrinsic motivation and educational relevance are, of course, widely recognised; but a didactic teacher does not have much scope for finding out how far they may apply in a specific case. One of the claimed advantages of the constructivist approach is that the two-way interaction between teacher and learner can reveal whether the tasks are stimulating and well-matched to the child's cognitive needs and ambitions.

Since the introduction of the National Curriculum (NC) in the UK, primary teachers have had to think, as never before, in terms of hierarchies of levels. There are two rather different concerns: differentiation for teaching and assessment. Both the Standard Assessment Tasks (SATs) and continuous Teacher Assessment are bound by the level descriptors published in the NC, and also by the allocation of knowledge and skills to specific key stages in the Programmes of Study. Some considerable anxiety has been generated by this requirement to allocate pupils to levels of performance, because the NC documents do not set out detailed criteria for each point of assessment (indeed to do so would require a thick directory for each subject), and so teachers have to make use of general principles.

There is a lesson to be learnt from the 1970s, when a misguided attempt to apply Piaget's 'stages' theory to classroom matters led to disappointment, and, for some, to the rejection of education theory altogether. Piaget had proposed a theory of cognitive development which included the hypothesis that the human mind acquired, mainly through experience, powers of logical thought. The ability to *imagine* acting upon the environment (rather than having to actually do so) he labelled 'concrete operational thought', and his own and subsequent research found that it was reached by most children somewhere after four or five years of age. The next stage, that of 'formal operations' (thinking with symbols or abstract relationships) was rarely reached before the age of 11. The theory was necessarily complex, and required care in its application to any individual child or task (see Chapter 11 for further discussion).

It was tempting to provide for teachers (especially teachers in training) a simplified version of Piaget's 'stages theory', reduced to about two pages, and to move on rather rapidly from the theory to its possible classroom applications (about which Piaget had written almost nothing). One common distortion was to assume that all children, except those with

Special Educational Needs (SEN), reached these stages at the same age (often six to seven years for concrete operations); another was that children would begin to use these mental abilities in all areas of knowledge simultaneously.

If only things were so simple! All we would need would be a set of graded exercises, and the child's birth certificate. Another false deduction from the theory was that since children developed through experience, they should not be 'taught' anything, but given the opportunity to 'discover' it. After the false hopes, the reaction came: teachers felt let down, and the message to students was that Piaget is useless.

Present opinion is that Piaget's theory is important and well-founded, though like all theories it may need to be revised, and that its sphere of application is more limited than was once assumed. Questioning children, or setting them tasks, to diagnose developmental level is tricky, and can lead to false or artificial results if the child is confused, or looking for unintentional prompts. Thinking by analogy may be more important than strictly logical (linear) reasoning. Lee *et al.* (1995) argue that it is in the area of second-order concepts (such as 'evidence' or 'change') rather than first-order concepts (i.e. specifics such as 'castle' or 'treaty') that progression might be measured.

But the principal revision which has had to be made to the popular form of progression theory is this: a person's powers of rationality are not context-free, but depend to an extent upon specific experience and factual

Figure 4 The 'ladders' analogy for cognitive development.

knowledge. And of course other important factors, besides rationality, affect learning: literacy, language fluency, and motivation, for example (see Chapter 4).

In other words, there may well be stages of cognitive growth, but every child climbs his own ladder, and what is more, finds the ladder steeper or less steep for different subjects or topics. There are no short cuts to diagnostic assessment.

Assessment

Meaningful learning can be helped by a constructivist approach to teaching, as will be discussed in the next chapter. The assessment of meaningful conceptual knowledge also needs something like a constructivist approach. For one thing, we must avoid at all costs the rote-learned answer, for this conceals rather than displays the child's real state of active knowledge. So the assessment task must call for some active operation with the knowledge being tested: maybe a statement, in new words, of how it would apply to some novel situation – an explanation or prediction. In this context, giving an explanation means answering the question, 'Try to think of a reason why so-and-so happened' rather than, 'What explanation can you remember being taught?'

Some people have argued that the only true evidence of a person's active possession of a conceptual scheme is to observe whether he/she will bring out and use that scheme when the circumstances require it. This is *uncued* testing, and although I think it is of great value in educational research, it requires considerable skill and patience, and may not find much of a role in teacher assessment. Perhaps the nearest approach to it in recent National Curriculum assessment was the first set of practical SATs in science and mathematics. But these had been introduced without adequate preparation or resourcing, and were quickly abandoned (in response to teachers' demands, according to the government) and replaced by paper-and-pencil tests which 'are likely to narrow rather than widen learning opportunities for children' (O'Hear and White 1993:124).

However, there is one component of teacher assessment known as the 'critical incident technique', which applies to the child's unplanned performance (SEAC 1990). If, during a normal lesson, you are surprised by a child's contribution or performance, either because it shows unexpected insight, or alternatively an unsuspected misunderstanding, you should immediately make a note of it and later enter the incident, with your analysis, into the child's assessment file.

13

Exercise 2.2 Children's alternative ideas

Study samples of children's work, and write a brief comment about each. Decide whether the ideas are (a) simplistic, and showing a need for teacher input; (b) clearly expressed, and presumably satisfactory to the child, but containing errors of interpretation, or assumptions that are contrary to 'received knowledge'; (c) approximations to the accepted adult knowledge.

In each case, make a judgement as to whether the work should be accepted, or whether any immediate 'corrections' are called for.

Exercise 2.3 A critical incident

Bring for group discussion a written account (100–200 words) of a 'critical incident' which you have observed in the classroom, which provided you with an insight into one child's level of understanding of a specific subject.

If possible, make a comparison of this with the National Curriculum (or Desirable Learning Outcomes) or other published criteria.

Exercise 2.4 Ready to learn?

Consider the question: 'Is it harmful, or at least a waste of time, to try to teach a child something before he/she is ready for it?'

Recall and relate incidents in your experience which illustrate the effect of confronting children with tasks which were too difficult for them; or cases of children being deliberately held back from work that they might have benefited from.

CHAPTER 3

Constructivist Teaching

Stages in the adoption of constructivist teaching methods
1. The novice teacher[1]

This section is addressed to a student or newly qualified teacher (NQT) who is still concerned to develop skills of teaching in the traditional didactic or transmission style. It may well be that this method is extensively used in her school, so she rightly feels that she must demonstrate her competence at it before going on to the more demanding techniques of differentiated or individualised teaching. I suggest that, despite these constraints, the constructivist approach can offer ways of achieving more efficient teaching.

For a start, instead of accepting a prescription (from textbook, teachers' guide or any printed curriculum) of what exactly is to be taught, the teacher can try to select the content to match the pupils' needs. This can initially be done at whole-class level:

* Consider what the children have shown an interest in, in the recent past.
* With regard to any proposed task, judge whether the skills which will be required are those which most of the children can reach (with your help, perhaps), but which they need to practise.

This is of course nothing more than normal lesson planning, and matching the task to the children's needs. But the addition of preliminary trials, or tests of what they know already, would give it a constructivist flavour.

This more systematic elicitation of *individual* children's existing knowledge and understanding of a concept will usually be revealing, in two ways: 1) the wide variety of views, and the range of sophistication; and 2) the great chasm between what many children know (or think they know) and what an educated person is expected to know.

---

1 The two stages which I am suggesting are defined as: 1) finding out children's ideas in order to be able to address errors and gaps, and help children to overcome them; and 2) planning activities which permit the children to clarify and communicate their own ideas, and to encounter a range of alternative views.

So, forewarned is forearmed. The teacher can use the detailed revelation of the children's errors, misconceptions and half-formed ideas as a basis for a more efficient teaching plan. She will now be able to avoid the pitfall of assuming any prerequisite knowledge (just because she has been told that the class has 'done it last year'). By finding out in advance what it is that the children know, she will have something real to build on. She will also avoid the opposite mistake of assuming the children know *nothing*, and so planning a tedious and unnecessarily simple introductory lesson.

'Start from what the children already know' is good advice, if you can find out where that is. But you must remind yourself that 'what they already know', for this purpose, means 'what they understand'. You cannot find this by a quick 'diagnostic test' if it tests only superficial recall of facts. In order to genuinely link up with what the pupils already know, you will start with a task that requires the pupils to *use* this knowledge.

In addition to 'private' elicitation strategies with one's own class, one can draw upon published research findings, as mentioned previously. These will reveal the kind of alternative conceptions found among children of a given age range, and will alert the teacher to the possibility that some children in her class may hold such views. She may also find this knowledge useful for diagnosing individual children's mistakes, and for setting up activities to help shift children's ideas towards the accepted ones.

After elicitation and diagnosis comes 'intervention'. When you have diagnosed some aspect of the child's understanding which seems weak or incomplete, you have to bring the child to a state of active attention to it. This may require questioning or a challenge (from the teacher or, preferably, another child). Some educationists have proposed setting up a 'cognitive conflict', that is, an awareness of a contradiction or anomaly between what the child would have expected or predicted and what is found to be the fact ('facts' can be presented from a book, a database or perhaps a practical investigation). The teacher's aim is to help the child move on, correct the mistaken notion, and adopt a more acceptable one.

Note, however, that this aim is traditional and 'transmissionist', despite the borrowing of some constructivist techniques. The teacher is still wedded to 'right answers', rather than to autonomous, high-quality thinking. It is still the teacher who is in charge of what is to be learned, and what knowledge is regarded as acceptable.

As I suggested at the start of this section, the use of constructivist techniques for didactic ends is only a halfway house, but it is still of value; and furthermore it may help to give the trainee or NQT some confidence in the approach. Figure 5 is a flow-chart showing the steps involved. You will recognise similarities with techniques which are recommended for the teaching of reading and arithmetic.

BASIC
estimate or assess the knowledge of the class. Plan tasks which match this.

↓

DIFFERENTIATE
take account of the range of ability within the class.
Plan tasks which allow children to work at their own level, with a range of cognitive outcomes.

↓

INDIVIDUALISED
assess (or be ready to notice) children's individual knowledge. (Note: published research findings may help you here.) Diagnose *specific* misunderstandings, and plan individual interventions (teaching, resources) to remedy these.

Figure 5 Steps in the introduction of constructivist methods into 'ordinary teaching'.

Exercise 3.1 Planned intervention

In Exercise 2.1 each student elicited the ideas of a co-student on a chosen topic. This exercise is to plan and conduct a short (ten minute) lesson, to remedy faults or extend knowledge.

In advance of the group session you should write a Lesson Plan, setting out the state of your partner's knowledge of the chosen topic, and proposing educational objectives for a 10–12 minute intervention, followed by a short (three minute) test, also prepared in advance. Students A and B should decide the order of their teaching, possibly by the toss of a coin, and then go ahead with it. Afterwards, discuss and write evaluations.

Were the objectives all achieved? Were they achievable, under the circumstances?

As a group activity, work in double pairs (as before).

Stages in the adoption of constructivist teaching methods 2. The more experienced teacher

The teacher who is comfortable with all the necessary techniques of planning, organisation, control of the class – and of time – may feel that the pupils' learning still leaves something to be desired. This disquiet may take the form of a recognition that pupils have become too dependent upon spoonfeeding: that is, they want to be told exactly what to do and what to learn. Another source of disquiet may be that although the pupils do what is expected of them and complete their tasks or exercises accurately, they do not contribute their own ideas, and do not extend or apply their learned knowledge in any personal way.

> Throughout my teaching history so far, I have noticed that children are always taught the correct procedure to tackle a problem [in maths], but are not taught the concept behind it. Children in schools are increasingly being geared towards getting the right answers … We are increasingly being so geared towards producing results and pushing up levels of standards that we are forgetting the needs of pupils.
>
> Student teacher, May 1998

It is then time for more radical constructivist teaching, with the aim of encouraging children to build sturdy, meaningful intellectual structures. Knowledge of this sort can (usually) withstand challenge, and can be called upon for use in the discussion of novel topics. Its value lies in the fact that it is not only correct, it is fruitful. It is valued by the possessor as something worth knowing.

The teaching method must reach into new, perhaps strange, territory: helping children to build and to sort out their ideas, without telling them what is right, or what to think. Three examples of strategies which illustrate this are:

The non-judgemental reception

The teacher, aiming to help some nine-year-olds to trust their own judgements as to the moral worth of some characters in a story, arranges small-group discussions. Afterwards the children tell what they have decided on, with their reasons (if they agree) or (if they cannot) the reasons why not. Our teacher, though hearing some unusual and very questionable opinions, decides not to impose her own views, even by stealth. Her reasoning is that there is too high a risk that *any* move on her part to oppose the children's conclusions will undermine their newly-established confidence in their own ability to grapple with ethical issues. So she chooses to allow the children to tell their own considered views, without telling them her own (this requires deliberate self-restraint!).

The non-committal reception

In another lesson the teacher is asking the class questions which require some recall of previous knowledge (geometry, say), and she receives an answer which is 'right', i.e. recognizably successful; but instead of acknowledging this, by saying 'Good', she takes it coolly ('OK') and proceeds by looking towards another table, saying in a neutral voice, 'Any other ideas?'; or perhaps 'Does anyone agree with [child's name]?' The rationale is that it is important to reduce the pupils' ambitions to be the first to give the right answer, like a contest; and one way to do this is to avoid giving praise exclusively to pupils who succeed at this 'game'. There is also the aim of making *all* the class think more deeply, by mildly challenging, for a moment, the correct answer. It is important not so much to be right, as to know what grounds one has for believing one's answer to be right (see also Metacognition).

Provisionally tolerant reception

A similar teaching strategy is to ask a question, and accept a suggestion for consideration even though it is flawed, by some phrase such as 'Right, that's an idea. Would you like to try it out (i.e. practically)?' Then, during the activity, she will find the opportunity to ask for a fuller account of the proposal, both from its author and from other pupils. Perhaps this interrogation will expose the fault, but again, perhaps not. It could even be that the method will turn out to work perfectly well, under the conditions.

Radical constructivism

Some teachers (and mentors) may feel suspicious of the statement of constructivist principle given a page back:

> ... helping children to build and to sort out their ideas, without telling them what is right, or what to think.

Isn't it the teacher's *job* to tell children what is right, and to help them to correct their mistakes? Most people would initially answer 'Yes'. But reflect a moment: perhaps rushing in with a correction or a ready-made 'right answer' is not the best way (Wadsworth 1997). Perhaps it is equally important to lead the child to question his/her knowledge at the point where the teacher sees a fault. Then the *need for change* will have been gener-ated, and the improvement will be accepted gratefully rather than grudg-ingly – or sycophantically.

Of course the teacher should draw attention to any faults or mistakes which the child is capable of recognising. If Martin has described Holland as an arid mountainous region, it would usually be right to challenge it right away, and vigorously. If Mona writes or says that the day after September 30 is September 31, this is not an 'alternative idea' which can be allowed to pass. (Perhaps 'Go and look on the calendar' might be appropriate – if there is one handy.)

But when Ben, a nine-year-old from Southampton, writes 'Southampton was important because it was the most important port for ships to America', I would let it go, even if it was factually inaccurate, and concentrate instead on what point Ben is trying to make, and what argument he is trying to build.

A moderate constructivist teacher would say that 'telling the child what is right' is to be applauded, on condition that (a) the version of 'what is right' has been selected in accordance with the child's ability and associated knowledge; and (b) that the child wants to know. It is the dogmatic transmission of some inappropriately difficult, adult-level answer that one would object to.

However, the extreme constructivist might object to *any* attempt by the teacher to force on the child an answer which did not 'seem right' to that child: and this would apply equally to inducement by 'bribery' in the form of praise or test marks for an insincere answer. The teacher's decision must respect the basic principle of the autonomy of the learner: students must always accept responsibility for the intelligibility, as well as the veracity, of what they learn.

We must be careful to be clear on just what the word 'truth' means to the radical constructivist. If we deny that absolute, objective truth exists, it might seem that 'anything goes' – that is, that whatever we choose to say is so, is so. But that is not constructivism, it is relativism; and I for one do not find it convincing. It seems to be an extension from the well-known fact that people differ in their aesthetic tastes, to an acceptance that all judgements are of equal worth. The relativist can be recognized by his infuriating habit of replying, to any assertion made as part of an argument, 'If you say so', or 'You're entitled to your view', without any attempt to refute it. It is an anti-rationalist position, and I doubt whether it has any place in education.

To the radical constructivist, a proposition *can* be right or wrong, true or false. But the criterion for truth is not a comparison with some imaginary absolute truth: rather, it is on the grounds of utility – whether the idea *works*. This may sometimes be simply pragmatic, or practical: the timetable is correct (at least in this one detail) if the train scheduled to arrive at 8.12 a.m. does arrive at 8.12 or soon after. In other cases there is no such empirical test, and truth means consistency with other knowledge, leading to the satisfaction of feeling that the situation is understood, and that everything is (cognitively) under control. These matters will be discussed more fully in Chapter 11.

Exercise 3.2 Are you a 'radical constructivist'?

Radical constructivism has been defined (by von Glasersfeld) as:

'... a theory of knowledge in which knowledge does not reflect an 'objective' ontological reality, but exclusively an ordering and organisation of a world constituted by our experience'

from which it follows that:

'... concepts, ideas and meanings cannot be [directly] transferred from one [person] to another, but must be abstracted from individual experience.'

In opposition to this, Matthews (1994: 154) argues:

'For the most part, individuals *learn*, not construct, meanings.'

Decide what your own position is. Are you persuaded that the teacher should act as stated at the start of this section (radical constructivism)? Or do you feel that the teacher has the right, and duty, to correct the pupils' misconceptions?

Prepare notes on your viewpoint, and your reasoning. Then discuss the issue with your group.

Metacognition

An important so-called study skill (though I think it is an attitude rather than a skill) is to be aware of how sure we are of what we know, and what our reasons are for believing it to be true. While it may have a place in helping students to learn, I am here concerned with how it can help teachers to teach. It will clearly make a difference to teaching style whether the content knowledge is felt to be convincing, and to have that 'ring of truth', or whether it is just school-book knowledge that happens to be on the syllabus.

Teachers often encounter a conflict situation when they are planning a medium-term scheme, if they become aware that their own understanding of some of the content is limited or hazy. To the traditional 'transmissionist' teacher there is but one right thing to do: to find a textbook, study the topic, and try to prepare a sufficiently simplified version for teaching to the class. This may be done somewhat grudgingly, with the pessimistic expectation that the pupils are unlikely to understand it (especially since their teacher can't), and so will just have to 'learn' it. There may also be some fear of having their ignorance exposed by a child's questions – one of the anxieties most commonly voiced by non-specialists. (This is considered in the next section.)

The constructivist teacher is in a happier position. For one thing, the process of 'learning together' is more respectable; and it is probable that the teacher will be able to keep ahead of the children in learning the topic. Secondly, the assumptions about the level of knowledge to be taught, even if based on the NC, may be mistaken, and impracticable for a given class. Specialists may have succeeded in tricking the teaching body into accepting that some area of knowledge is an essential item in primary education, even though it is actually very difficult. The constructivist teacher is in a good position to recognise this, and to choose a more suitable version to present to the class.

A notorious example of advanced knowledge, which primary teachers have been led to believe it is their duty to teach, is forces and energy. Obviously this section of physics (mechanics) deals with many common and well-known experiences in the natural and technological worlds, so the children are entitled to some education about it. But unfortunately the topic is overshadowed by the GCSE programme, with its tightly-defined concepts of force, momentum, mass, inertia, gravitational field, etc., all guarded by secondary physics specialists watching like hawks for any misuse of these terms. (This theme will be taken up again in Chapter 6.)

The dilemma arises if teachers take the syllabus (National Curriculum Programmes of Study or NC PoS) as given and unquestionable. They may then find that they have set themselves the task of teaching something which they know (or will soon find) that their pupils cannot understand. The way to avoid this trap is to apply the pedagogic principles from this section, especially the priority of the *useability* of a concept by the learner, rather than some sterile objective 'correctness'.

Questioning

Teachers do a lot of questioning, but numerous researchers have remarked that much of it is unhelpful in any educational sense. In this category we can include questions that merely check up on recall of facts ('What is the capital of Australia?'), and indeed most 'closed' questions (those which have only one acceptable answer). It is strange that teachers spend so much time asking questions to which they obviously know (or think they know) the answer already. This is not regarded as a healthy practice in any normal social environment, and can try the patience of your friends (look what happened to Socrates!). The over-use of this 'assessment mode' of questioning helps to make school seem unrelated to real life.

Beyond this peculiar practice of asking children questions which they know you know, there may be a problematic aspect to this teachers' habit of asking factual questions, even when they do not know the answer in advance and are not therefore setting a test; and this is that they are trivialising the child's contribution, and wasting the opportunity for encouraging thought. Shirley Maxwell (in Robson and Smedley 1996:4) gives the example of a teacher who asked a young child, who was telling the class of her experience of a pony ride, 'What colour were the ponies?' This seemingly innocuous question actually asserted the teacher's right to check up on the factual accuracy of the story, and (even more damagingly) suggested that facts, not feelings, were the aspects that were valued in her classroom.

It is not enough, then for a question to be 'open'. A fruitful question must permit, or rather engender, a thoughtful and original contribution. The teacher should avoid the role of tester, and should instead act the part of an interested and appreciative listener. David Wood (in Light 1991:115) suggests that if teachers reduce the frequency of their questions, and instead 'offer contributions which are high in their level of presentation (e.g. speculations, opinions, reasoning etc.), children are likely to respond in kind.'

It seems likely that children would open up, and make spontaneous and sincere suggestions, if only the teacher would stop trying to control the cognitive procedure so tightly. Think of the more conversational questioning style typical of parents talking with their children, and compare it with the arrogant, interrogative style so often adopted by teachers. No wonder many children prefer to keep quiet at school (see Exercise 3.3 on Questioning).

Children's questions

It can be beneficial to ask the pupils, as an exercise, to think up (and if feasible write down) their own questions about the topic of the current lesson. They will, of course, need some training in this, because at first their questions will probably be closed and factual; but in time they can be shown how to formulate useful questions that contribute to a growth in their own understanding.

It is up to the teacher to decide whether to give a direct answer to these questions, or to encourage the children to embark upon investigations. Time, resources, and the nature of the question will dictate the choice.

I have already mentioned that trainee teachers often feel anxious about being 'caught out' by a child's question to which they do not know the authoritative answer. Generally these fears are groundless, if the constructivist approach has been adopted, because the 'answer' (which the teacher doesn't know) would probably be unsuitable anyway. The best thing to do is to explore more fully what the child knows already, and what question is really intended. (This applies especially to questions beginning 'Why?', which often mean 'Tell me more about …', rather than calling for a complicated explanation.) In any case, the answer the child needs will turn out to be far simpler than the 'expert' (GCSE or A-level) one. I would generally advise you not to attempt to give any explanation that is not known to most of the adult population, except in the case of an unusually able child pursuing a special interest.

Conversation about events and observations

One of the most powerful strategies for helping pupils to construct successful knowledge resembles that used for the elicitation of firmly-held concepts: i.e. open-minded conversation or exploration of meaning. It helps if the conversation is centred on or anchored to some event or observation which pupil and teacher can share. Your role is to ask for an explanation of 'what is going on here', and to be a neutral but intelligent listener. You should initially probe the child's ideas, in a non-judgemental way; but you may remark upon inconsistencies, and correct errors of fact.

In other words, you are helping the child to build up the best possible version of his/her model, and to test it against experience. If this model has limitations (i.e. is 'wrong' in relation to the official version), the weaknesses will eventually show, and the learner may decide to abandon the weaker model and switch allegiance to the stronger (and probably more difficult) model. But this may well be a lengthy process, not to be achieved today.

In some cases it may be useful to bring about some 'cognitive conflict', by drawing attention to a discrepancy between some consequence or prediction from the child's model, and some other known or demonstrable fact. But take care: the episode may not end, as you desire, with the child shifting from his/her current model to your preferred one. It can happen that the confused child abandons all hope of understanding the situation at all. Teaching, if clumsily done, can sometimes destroy knowledge without putting anything in its place.

Exercise 3.3 Questioning

Study the following excerpts from Tizard and Hughes (1984, pp. 190–225) of nursery teachers talking with four-year-olds. Consider the purpose, and the outcome, of the questions.

Count up the number of questions asked by (a) teachers, (b) children.

1. Rolling clay

Joyce, aged four, is rolling out clay, and the teacher has come to sit by her.

1. Teacher: What's that going to be, Joyce? [No reply] ... How are you making it?
2. Child: Rolling it.
3. Teacher: You're rolling it, are you? Isn't that lovely? Oh, what's happening to it when you roll it?
4. Child: Getting bigger.
5. Teacher: Getting bigger. Is it getting fatter?
6. Child: Yeah.
7. Teacher: Is it? Or is it getting longer?
8. Child: Longer.
9. Teacher: Longer. Are my hands bigger than your hands?
10. Child: My hands are little.
11. Teacher: Your hands are little, yes.
12. Child: It's getting bigger. Getting long. And long. Look!
13. Teacher: Mmmm. What's happened to it, Joyce?
14. Child: Got bigger.
15. Teacher: It has. My word!

2. Sweets

The teacher is reading a book called *Big Sweets and Little Sweets* to a group of children. She asks Lynne a question.

21. Teacher: What sorts of sweets do you like?
22. Child: Lots of sweets.
23. Teacher: Lots of them? Do you like any of them specially?
24. Child: I've got some indoors.
25. Teacher: Have you? What kind?
26. Child: Got a packet.
27. Teacher: A packet of them? What, Smarties?
28. Child: They're in a bag.
29. Teacher: In a bag? Smarties are in a box, aren't they?
30. Teacher: [after reading some more of the book] What's the word for all kinds of jelly babies and Smarties? ... We say 'I'm going to buy some ———' [Implied request to Lynne to fill in the missing word.]
31. Child: [indignantly] I *have* had some Smarties.
32. Teacher: Can you think of the word?

33. Child: [persists] But I *have* had some Smarties.
34. Teacher: What kind of shop do you go and buy Smarties from?
35. Child B: A children's shop.
36. Teacher: [waits]
37. Child C: No, a sweetie shop.
38. Teacher: [approvingly] A *sweet* shop. [Proceeds to read book.]

3. Paint.
The teacher joins a girl who announces:

41. Child: I did a painting, a long one.
42. Teacher: You and Joan?
43. Child: Mm. [In fact the two girls had *not* been painting together.]
44. Teacher: What colour did you paint with?
45. Child: I had red and blue, dark blue.
46. Teacher: Blue, isn't it? [Looking at the turquoise paint on the girl's arm, jokes] I don't think you painted a picture, I think you painted yourself!
47. Child: I *did* paint a picture. [Pause] That looks like green. [She looks at her arm, which has red and turquoise paint on it.]
48. Teacher: Green? No, that's red – look, there it is.
49. Child: Yeah. That looks like blood running out of my arm, doesn't it? [Points to red paint on arm.]
50. Teacher: Yes, you're bleeding aren't you? Does that one look like blood? [Points to turquoise paint on arm.]
51. Child: Mm.
52. Teacher: Mm? Is that the right colour for blood? What's that colour?
53. Child: [Doesn't answer.]

1. To what extent did the teacher's questions provoke thought?
2. Study turns 5-8; why does the girl agree with both suggestions? Does she really think that the clay is increasing in volume? See turn 14.
3. Why does the child evade the questions at turns 30 and 32? Why does the teacher wait, at 36?
4. What were the reasons for the children's wrong answers, or failure to answer, when they probably did know? See turns 10; 24 and 26; 43, and 51.
5. What does turn 49 suggest about the child's language ability?

CHAPTER 4

Motivation

It may seem strange to find a chapter on this subject, separated from those on teaching and learning. So perhaps I should declare that I am not implying that it is an optional aspect of teaching that can be added later, after basic techniques have been mastered. On the contrary, it is fundamental from the start that we attempt to find which of our teaching approaches result in good motivation. Yet many student teachers find that their preoccupation with management and learning objectives, and particularly with *outcomes*, makes them oblivious to motivation issues until they are confronted by the crisis situation of an obviously *un*motivated group of children.

A common and perhaps rather glib reaction is to declare that all lessons should be 'fun'. I have seen activities in lesson plans justified by no more than that they are 'a fun thing to do'. I hesitate to agree that all 'fun' activities have an educational value. Dressing up in bright clothes and eating trifle and cream is fun, but it could not be justified as a classroom activity more often than once a year. And sometimes 'having fun' is a malicious activity, involving the attempted humiliation of other people (other pupils, or the teacher). The more common danger, however, is that 'fun' may turn out to be an undemanding substitute for worthwhile work: 'a bit of a laugh', in fact. It can be used by the teacher as an inducement to conformity, or to reward children for accepting, without complaining, some apparently futile busy-work.

Motivation to learn is more subtle than this: it is a deep-seated pleasure in personal achievement, mental growth, and competence.

Some motivating strategies seem no more than just good teaching, e.g. making sure that all children 'get their turn', or their opportunity to get involved. Equally, most teachers know the value of a certain amount of novelty, both in lesson content and in the type of activity.

Exercise 4.1 Motivation

1. Quickly make a list of eight or more different causal factors for pupils' motivation towards school learning activities. Attempt to classify these as either extrinsic or intrinsic motivation.
2. Consider whether any of these might be a hindrance to education, rather than a help.
3. Consider your own practice as a teacher. Are you sure that the motivating strategies which you employ are all benign?

Some children will work alone, engrossed on some task, for hours. Should we leave well alone? Or should we intervene, to help the child to gain more from the activity? Some children need to communicate their thoughts without delay. They seem to need you to go along every five minutes, to approve and re-motivate – otherwise they will leave off, and go to distract someone else.

Extrinsic motivation

Approval by adults (teacher, parents) is a powerful motivator, but I regard it as extrinsic to the pupil's personal learning and development. There is a danger that teachers – and indeed the whole education system – will exploit children's love of approval as a motivation for school work which otherwise would seem pointless and demotivating. Why else should children struggle to copy the letters of the alphabet, or the numbers 1 to 10? Why else should 'all walk in a straight line, on tip-toe, quiet as mice'?

Is this desire to conform, which teachers trade on so much, an intrinsic intuition, or a social habit imposed by the school? Is it solely a desire to please, or a fear of displeasing or even of punishment?

A similar motivating factor is **competition**, and some schools encourage pupils to compare their marks or achievement levels by means of published lists. This has been more prevalent in secondary schools with grammar school ambitions, but is now to be found in primary schools, perhaps as a result of the SATs. Some maths or reading schemes consist of graded exercises or booklets, and the pupils know the order of progression, and judge themselves and others by their book number or colour. The sense of success on completing a unit in such a scheme can outweigh the meagre educational value of the contents. Some children hurry to complete their allotted 'reader' in order to get their tick on the record sheet, and then get on to some 'real' reading.

The problem here of course is that for every winner there must be a loser. It is doubtful whether being labelled a slow learner, or 'still at Level 1' at the end of Year 2, is an effective motivating factor.

Equally serious is the possibility that tests, which invariably measure outcome rather than method (product rather than process), will tempt teachers to pay attention only to this in class, too. They will look at a child's finished work, and judge it a success or failure, and as an indicator of learning[1]. They will pay less attention to a child's thought processes, including the reasons why the output was different from the approved one.

The constructivist teacher does not make the mistake of judging only the outcome. She will spend most of the time with children while they are still working towards a solution to the task, and will try to engage with the process of each child's cognitive activity (see Drummond 1993:89).

Relevance

I have left until last this rather elusive feature of motivation. It is difficult to classify as intrinsic or extrinsic, because although the relation between the curriculum and the child's individual interests is an intrinsic factor, the teacher's selection of content is often based on a stereotypical assumption as to what these interests might be.

Most primary teachers would claim to base their teaching on the child's experience; but they construe this 'experience' largely in terms of the everyday practical world in which children live. As Kieran Egan (1988:20) points out, this ignores the child's world as transfigured by fantasy. A similar concern exists for older pupils, whose world must include emotional and aesthetic experiences (e.g. a sense of wonder at the natural world) which a plain account of their 'environment' would omit.

I am not competent to pursue any further this glimpse of the child's world of emotions and imagery. Instead, I would suggest that we ought to try to appreciate just how much 'experience' involves 'making sense'. We risk trivialising the child's stock of experience if we treat it as just factual (houses, cars, the playground, food). Experience goes beyond recollection of physical activity: it also consists of reflective thought, learning, development of concepts, and understanding of causal relationships (both physical and social). Experience can be value-laden, leading to loving or loathing, fascination or fear, or anger. It is more than just information about the world.

So if motivation to learn is to arise from 'relevance', you have to be quite adventurous in divining what that consists of. For one thing, the task must

---

1 One of my most vivid personal memories of primary school is the dismay and anger (real tears dropping into my bottle of milk) occasioned, at around eight years, by my teacher's manner of conveying her opinion of my arithmetical performance. During the morning break ('milk time') she had returned to us, without comment, our marked exercise books; and I was confronted by a set of 20 red crosses, one against each of the 20 subtraction sums. But I survived it, didn't I? Probably did me good!

be meaningful in the sense that the child can conceive of a situation in which its performance would serve some real purpose. And secondly, it must be challenging – not trivial, repetitive, or totally predictable.

If it occurs to you that it would take an omniscient being to know exactly what task would be 'relevant' to each of 30 pupils, it follows that no mere teacher can ever succeed, unless:

a) the task is to some extent open; or

b) there is some choice as to which task to attempt.

If we provide a means for pupils to make an input (e.g. to provide their own examples, or to select the problem in the setting which most appeals to them), there is a greater chance of making the link between our intentions and their dispositions.

CHAPTER 5

Working Within a National Curriculum

> Child psychology was largely ignored in the construction of the National Curriculum.
>
> Kenneth Baker (1991), former Secretary of State for Education

It is essential that teachers should reconcile the constructivist approach with their relevant National Curriculum or other mandatory guidelines. It is most unlikely that any fundamental incompatibility will be found, but it may well be necessary to re-examine certain customs and interpretations, and particularly to clarify and perhaps reappraise the assumptions as to goals.

The National Curriculum for England and Wales is definitely a specification of a minimum syllabus (or entitlement) of content, and not of the teaching methodology (or means of delivery): see, e.g., 'Medium-term planning' in SCAA (1995a:10). Generally this content is presented as programmes of study covering two distinct areas: (1) knowledge and understanding; and (2) skills and processes.

In mathematics the latter component is found in the section 'Using and applying mathematics', which includes the requirement that pupils should '... explain their thinking to support the development of their reasoning'[1].

In addition, generic skills and attitudes are stated, such as: '... take increasing responsibility for organising and extending tasks; devise and refine their own ways of recording; *ask questions and follow alternative suggestions*' (my emphasis).

A similar process, 'Interpreting history', requires pupils to 'identify and *give reasons for different ways* in which the past is represented and interpreted' (my emphasis).

In science we find the following approaches to theorising: at KS2: 'obtain evidence to test scientific ideas in a variety of ways'; leading on to:

---

1 DfE (1995) *Mathematics in the National Curriculum*, HMSO, p.,2. The next quotes are from Maths p. 6, History p.5, and Science pp. 7 & 14.

'consider the importance of evidence and creative thought in the development of scientific theories'.

It is clear, then, that a pluralistic view of knowledge is allowed by the National Curriculum Programmes of Study.

The new requirements for courses of Initial Teacher Training (as the British government has chosen to call it) specify in considerable detail how the core subjects should be taught. In mathematics many traditional techniques are prescribed (see DfEE (1998a) Circular no. 4/98, especially pp. 53–5), which could give the impression that a transmission mode of teaching is being recommended. But there are also quite a number of strategies with which the constructivist would agree: e.g. the use of 'high quality, interactive oral work', and teaching which will 'enable pupils to contribute actively to discussion' (p. 56). Teachers are urged to: 'use interactive methods with whole classes, groups and individuals, including ... open and closed, oral and written questions which elicit answers from which pupils' mathematical understanding can be judged.' There is a full section entitled 'Common errors and misconceptions in mathematics' which will help student-teachers to recognise ways in which these arise (including careless teaching!). Some of these points will be considered further in Chapter 9. Recent government initiatives in the teaching of language – the so-called Literacy Hour – have seemed to some observers to be prescriptive, inflexible, onerous and obsessed with fastidious syntax at the expense of semantic effectiveness. I think, however, that this would be an over-reaction. It is possible for teachers to train pupils in the mechanics of language (spelling, punctuation, vocabulary) for part of the lesson, using a transmission technique, and then to change to helping children to appreciate the meaning and purpose of language for the next twenty minutes. The mistake would be to try to combine these disparate aims in a single activity. The Literacy Strategy documentation (DfEE 1998b) contains many objectives in the text-level strand of the Framework, which can only be achieved by a constructivist approach. Literate Primary pupils should, it says on p. 3:

- have an interest in words and their meanings
- be interested in books ... and evaluate and justify their preferences
- through reading and writing, develop ... imagination, inventiveness and critical awareness.

More specifically, in Year 1 term 2 children will 'discuss reasons for, or causes of, incidents in stories', and 'discuss characters [and] speculate about how they might behave'. In Year 5 term 1, children should not only write their own playscript, but 'evaluate script *and performance* for their dramatic interest and impact' (my italics). We shall look further into this new initiative in Chapter 7. It reinforces the requirement of the NC for

English, KS2 target 5(e), to conduct 'oral and written activities which require pupils to make critical and imaginative responses to ... literature'.

More problematic for the constructivist teacher is the system of assessment, and in particular the Standard Assessment Tasks, because these have been seen in some quarters as being distinctly prescriptive in tone. For example, the mark schemes for some SATs have rewarded knowledge only if it is expressed in certain approved vocabulary. So there is a risk that pupils who have been guided towards a firm understanding of some concept, appropriate for their age, may be given little or no credit for this on a standard test[1].

The teacher's, and equally importantly the school's, response to this kind of difficulty must be formulated after very careful consideration. Some possible contributions to such a debate are shown in the box overleaf.

When it comes to planning a course of study for a specified topic, an important feature of the medium-term plan (or scheme of work) is to identify all the ideas (concepts, theories, definitions, special skills) which may prove difficult to some pupils. It is frequently necessary to research the children's existing state of knowledge, in order to decide what will be appropriate provision of material, examples, texts and exercises. Planning for pupils' participation must be at least as thorough as for a transmission lesson.

There is a danger with any 'topic-based' curriculum which must be faced up to by a constructivist teacher, and that is 'lack of rigour'. The attack takes the form of the claim that pupils engaged on topic work miss out on engagement with the characteristic concepts and intellectual methods which belong to academic disciplines (i.e. separate subjects). The constructivist teacher, in the habit of working with children's personal opinions, may be accused of encouraging sentiment and sloppy thinking instead of careful argument based on factual evidence and accepted theory. Clearly this need not be so, but it is something to guard against. A balance must be reached between breadth and quality of intellectual development. To make a quick self-diagnosis, try counting up the number of 'higher-order' questions you ask. (These require the pupil to think both creatively and rationally; but while this sounds demanding, with suitable topics they can be found even for young children.)

Behind most items in the syllabus there is hidden some cognitive obstacle, and it is the teacher's responsibility to help each child to confront it and, if possible, to move towards a better understanding. Sometimes

---

1 For example 'Children were unfamiliar with the degree of accuracy required ... or using the correct scientific term.' 'Many children lost potential marks where in the same question they responded both with the scientifically correct and a scientifically incorrect answer.' SCAA (1995b:29). Further examples are in Selley (1998).

1. 'Priorities'
The child's education and mental development must take precedence over tests. The teacher's duty is to teach as well as possible, and there are other pedagogic goals to be pursued, apart from the tests. The child's confidence, attitude to learning, and self-esteem need to be considered, as do cooperation and communication between pupil and teacher.

2. 'Formative assessment'
The teacher will, as a matter of routine, be conducting frequent informal testing, which will provide a detailed profile for each pupil and will form the basis for planning. The formal reporting of this information constitutes the Teacher Assessment, and this should be regarded as more valid (though not necessarily more reliable) than the SATs. However, the school should welcome the standard tests as an additional source of information about the child's progress, to supplement the Teacher Assessment. Apart from familiarising the children with the style of the tests, no further action need be taken. If, when the marked tests are returned to the school, the teacher detects marking errors arising from failure to give due credit for correct answers expressed in an unexpected way, the total mark can be amended for internal use (it will rarely affect a whole Level).

3. 'Long-term goals'
Knowledge and understanding acquired by a constructive learning process will be more secure than similar knowledge learned superficially. Therefore the pupil's progress will be greater in the long run. This may show up as an enhanced performance on the SATs (despite the objections mentioned above); and even if not, it will lead to success at a later stage. This may well enhance the school's reputation, especially with the staff at the child's next school.

4. 'Morale'
Students who enjoy their lessons are likely to be better behaved than those who are frustrated or bored. Constructivist teaching methods make great demands on the teacher's skills and expertise, but may pay off through reduced stress and anxiety.

Four arguments in defence of constructivist teaching,
against attack from advocates of itemised tests.

pupils experience difficulty with an idea because it has been assumed that some prerequisite idea has already been mastered. So it may, at times, be found necessary to go back to an easier example of the principle – perhaps one that 'should have' been learned one or two years before – and study it again. Sometimes drawing attention to the underlying similarity of the cases will be helpful (an example of metacognition).

Constructivist teaching can be expected to ensure that the *processes* are learned (or acquired) properly, since they will be experienced frequently during the study of the content. Relatively little of the factual knowledge in the PoS will be transmitted without undergoing the student's careful consideration, so the learning will usually provide practice at the mental skills associated with the subject.

However, a word of warning may be necessary here. If pupils are to develop generic intellectual skills (such as critical appraisal, or planning investigations, or just classification), they must be given the opportunity to do so in contexts which they already understand well. We must beware of the 'discovery learning fallacy', that a pupil can, unaided, discover or appraise new ideas at a higher level of cognitive demand. The constructivist teaching method is one in which the teacher works in close collaboration with the learner; it is not a self-teaching method.

Keeping up with the syllabus

The teacher, or student teacher, may feel under pressure to complete the teaching of a topic by some given date. The reasons for this may be that the school plan requires a move to another topic, or that it is expected that the class will keep parallel with another class, or that all pupils in that year have to be ready for a common test. The class working in the constructivist manner may seem to be taking too long to cover the topic, because the learning methods, being so thorough, are necessarily slow.

One way out of this difficulty is compromise. If time is running out, and there is material on the syllabus still untaught, then you should recognise that it cannot be taught constructively, and instead 'teach' it very quickly, by superficial transmission. As long as there is no pressure on the pupils to memorise the information, the brevity of the exposure will do no harm. In fact, for some it may be a welcome broadening of their experience. The 'quick look' is a common way of meeting knowledge for the first time.

If you feel guilty because your class has not written much about a topic (possibly because they have used their time talking about it instead), the accusingly empty space in the books can be filled quickly by various means: (1) stick in photocopied notes, or a text passage to be marked with coloured pens; (2) a large and simple drawing or chart copied from the board and completed individually by labelling or gap-filling; (3) if appropriate, by sticking in realia (food labels from foreign countries, holiday postcards, railway timetables, foreign coins as samples of different metals) and writing explanatory labels[1].

Alternatively, you might summarise the discussion by words on the board, write up the title, then give the class half an hour to write their own version. They should do this without further recourse to you, because you will be busy acting as scribe for the poor writers (or helping them at the word-processor).

Many of the apparent objections to constructivist teaching will disappear when it is realised that no-one is expected to employ the method exclusively (you cannot play golf with only one club). Some skills, such as handwriting or ball-throwing, may be taught by demonstration and imitation. Singing, French, cooking, measuring, woodwork: many school activities will continue as always, and owe little to constructivist methodology.

Remember that the strength of the method is that whatever is learned is learned well. But it follows that those who are still learning will not be able to demonstrate success, on a superficial assessment, since they will not be skilled at pretending to have learned. This means less outward show of learning; and so the teacher's confidence in her own ability to know that learning has occurred is vitally important. Equally so is her ability to assert this judgement to colleagues.

---

1 This suggestion has been rebuked as 'cheap'; but I say that if 'the system' makes unjustified demands for written work, even from Years 2 to 4, then it deserves such evasions.

Objections to Constructivist Teaching
(a) Elementary

A teacher who is attempting to introduce this method into a school where it is not yet well-established may meet with objections from colleagues and parents. I believe that any reader who has progressed this far in this book will have little difficulty in refuting them.

1. *Covering the curriculum.* If we leave it to the children to learn what they choose to, they will fail to learn what they need to.
2. *Speed.* There is a curriculum to be covered in limited time. If we allow the pace to be set by the slowest learners, we will never get it done. Alternatively, if we let children learn at their own speed, some will be slower than 'they' (the authority figures) expect, and so the exam results will suffer.
3. *Discipline.* If we allow the children to do as they please, they will become rowdy and disobedient.
4. *Noise.* If we allow – let alone encourage – children to talk during lessons, the classroom will be unbearably noisy. This is tiring and stressful for those children who prefer to work in silence.
5. *Back to basics.* There are basic skills, including writing, numeracy, and common-sense knowledge, that have to be taught thoroughly before we can afford the luxury of letting pupils follow their personal choices. The Literacy Hour, for example, does not allow pupils to choose what to read.

Exercise 5.1 Holding firm?
Prepare brief written responses to each of these objections. Then, working in groups of five, each student in turn opens the discussion.

Objections to Constructivist Teaching
(b) Advanced

'We have tried it before, and the experiment failed.' Ten years ago we had the New Maths, which was all about teaching children to understand mathematical operations, (and 'sets' and 'probability') instead of how to get their sums right. As a result, we have a 'lost generation' of school-leavers who do not know their multiplication tables, and cannot do division without using an electronic calculator. (Similar reference could be made to Nuffield Science, or the Schools Council Humanities Project.)

Note: these objections are the most difficult for the beginning teacher to deal with, because they allude to alleged historical evidence, not personal experience. One line of defence is to point out that although these innovative courses were distinctly process-centred, they were not necessarily constructivist, so the course material may not have been understood by the pupils (or their parents).

Part II
Specific Subject Studies

CHAPTER 6

Primary Science

Science is the subject area in which by far the most research on constructivism has been done (e.g. Driver 1985, Shapiro 1994, Osborne 1990). Perhaps one reason for this is that the content of the secondary school science curriculum is full of concepts which run counter to 'intuitive' or common-sense notions, and pupils often have difficulty in learning them. Until fairly recently, the assumption among teachers was that this could be overcome by more effective exposition ('explanation') of the ideas, together with suitable demonstrations and, of course, hard work. There was no lack of evidence that students often held mistaken ideas or misconceptions (test results showed this all too clearly), but the traditional strategy was to ignore these ideas (which, being 'wrong', were judged to be useless), and to try to present the 'correct' science in a way that could be learned: i.e. memorised.

In the 1960s a bold pedagogical experiment was carried out: the Nuffield Science Teaching Project. The basic principle was the belief that pupils would understand (and hence remember) concepts and generalisations which they discovered for themselves. Science lessons of this kind would be largely practical, and performed by the pupils (in pairs) rather than demonstrated by the teacher. A challenging question would be set (from the Teachers' Guide), and an investigation would be performed, using apparatus provided and fairly detailed instructions. The pupils' main input was supposed to be in the interpretation of results, leading to a clear and correct understanding of the science theory ('I do and I understand'). This was the guided discovery method.

It is now generally agreed (Solomon 1980:146) that the experiment failed, perhaps because the learning theory was basically flawed. The guided discovery exercises were designed to lead to important knowledge, and so they were inevitably too difficult for the majority of the students. Only the most able, the fastest learners, were quick-thinking enough to pick up the clues coming from the books and the teacher's 'guidance', and arrive at the intended knowledge. Most of the rest were frustrated ('I do and I am even more confused', as one cynic put it), and had to wait until the teacher put them straight at the end – if there was any time left. The lesson from this bit of history is that it is a mistake to try to combine investigation (a skill or process) with the learning of important, predetermined content.

One of the danger areas for this is in elementary physics, where the teacher (and some teachers' guides) can easily assume that the theory is so obvious that the pupils are bound to 'see' it, as soon as they come to inspect their practical results. I think that the following example casts sufficient doubt on this assumption.

Research (Millar & Lubben 1996) involving about 100 Year 4 and Year 6 children set them the problem of finding out the best insulating wrapping for keeping a can of cold drink cold. They were asked to predict whether a thick layer or a thin layer of the material (e.g. cloth) would be most effective. About one-third predicted thicker, one-third thinner, and the other third were unclear (or didn't know). After the practical work, using cans, thermometers, and ice-cold water, they got various results: some showing the intended result, that two layers of insulation led to a slower temperature rise than one, but almost as many getting the opposite. Some of the children who had predicted that the thicker layer would be the better insulator now, in the light of the refuting evidence, changed their minds. (The main source of error seems to have been the practice of paying heed only to the final temperatures reached after a set time – say 15 minutes – and ignoring the initial temperatures, which were not necessarily the same for each run.)

Equally interesting, to my mind, are those children who predicted that the thicker insulation would lead to faster warming, and who held to this theory even when their practical results were in conflict with it. They had good reasons for their unorthodox prediction: as one child explained, 'The thicker layers will trap more air, which will give heat to the can'. The results did not confirm this, so the results must be wrong! This showed, I would suggest, an admirable scepticism about school experiments, and is a valid attitude which is closer to that of the scientists than is the instant acceptance of hastily-obtained 'facts'.

I would love to know the origin of the children's 'warm air' theory, but the researchers did not have the time or opportunity to probe that deeply. I can only suggest that it grew from the well-known experience that we put on thicker clothes (or multiple layers) to keep warm, and that the child surmised that the trapped air in these clothes *generated* the resultant warmth.

I think it is pretty clear that if the children are to learn the theory of heat insulation through doing this experiment, they will not do so by inspecting their results (especially if these are erroneous), but by discussing their interpretations with their teacher during the practical session. Only if the teacher is prepared to listen to their ideas, and to adjudicate between expectations and results, will the learning outcome make the time and effort of the practical worthwhile.

The main point of this section is to emphasise the difference between the teaching of the skills of investigation (Sc1 – which will be considered below), and the use of practical experience to help the development of science knowledge and understanding (Sc2–4). They each require a different teaching strategy, as well as a different attitude on the part of the children, and it is probably wise not to mix them in the same lesson[1].

Alternative conceptions

Some children's conceptions (or explanatory ideas) are idiosyncratic, and unlike anyone else's. But on the whole they are just variants of popular ideas, well-known in our culture, though sometimes disparaged as 'outdated' or just plain wrong.

It is helpful to use the label 'model' for any imagined system which can provide explanations for experience. A model is a conceptual scheme, and it may be quite grand (e.g. the life cycle) or rather modest (e.g. 'homes'). Of course any model can be added to, or refined, so that it becomes better at explaining the known facts; so, over the course of some years, we may improve our models almost out of recognition. But some models, though satisfactory for the child, cannot be improved to a form which the adult (especially the specialist) will be satisfied with, and in these cases it is necessary, at some point in one's education, to abandon the simpler (or just more familiar) model, and adopt another one. This is progression.

A clear example of a child's alternative model, which illustrates this state of being wrong yet partly right, is shown in Figure 6. The idea seems to be that evaporation is the sucking up of water by clouds, in much the same way as a liquid drink can be sucked up.

Unfortunately, in the past some science teachers, perhaps influenced by an exaggerated respect for what they were told was the truth, came to regard popular (literally 'vulgar') knowledge as unworthy of any place in the school curriculum. (I regard this as closely comparable with the attitude of many music teachers, some 20 years ago, that jazz, let alone pop, had no place in the classroom.) So, instead of allowing pupils to talk about their

---

1 The National Curriculum for England and Wales (1995) contains four sections or 'Attainment Targets' for Science, which are often referred to, informally, as Sc1–4.

science experiences using the homely models which they already held in mind, these teachers tried to insist on the use of the official textbook theories or models. These were taught as if they were exclusively correct. The intellectual snobbery which lay beneath this was presumably unrecognised.

Of course, many students went through the system without much harm, and came out at 18 with a love of and an enthusiasm for this strict, exact science. From this number were drawn the next generation of secondary school science teachers. These in turn tried to impart the same attitude to their pupils, even those who were not destined to become science specialists. The latter were often left in a most unhappy state, of not understanding the 'expert' science very well, but believing that it was the only acceptable version.

This is the damaging attitude which I hope to expunge, especially among prospective primary teachers. They should not be so much in awe of expert science that they cannot use the children's 'alternative' models for the purpose of science conversation in the classroom.

Figure 6 A six-year-old's account of what happens
when water in a bowl evaporates (from Russell and Watt 1990).

Floating and sinking

This is a marvellous source of activity leading to scientific thinking, including predicting, classifying, hypothesis-testing, and explaining. The phenomenon of buoyancy (i.e. the property of either rising to the top of the liquid or sinking to the bottom when submerged) is quite rare in that it obeys a two-valued logic. Yes or no. Up or down. (This is unlike most properties, such as tall-short, or sweet-sour, which are continuous, and admit intermediate states.) Of course some objects float high in the water, while others may be almost below the surface: but these refinements can be ignored with infants, leaving the simple choice between float or sink. (Of course we can cheat the buoyancy rule by shaping the material into a boat, and this is valuable knowledge in itself: but the theoretical explanation is considerably more advanced than that for buoyancy, so we shall leave it for now.)

How many teachers around the world are, this very hour, asking young children to predict which things will float and which will sink? Thousands, I dare say. Their objectives will usually be unstated, but will include the development of the child's concept of buoyancy. The first to investigate such ideas systematically, and to publish his findings, was Jean Piaget (1930); and, as is well known, he identified a pre-operational thinking stage at which children were not basing their answers on any general theoretical understanding. They tended to guess, and give pseudo-reasons such as, 'This stick will float because it is long', even after they had seen a long knife sink; or, 'The nail will sink because it is pointed'.

Whether or not we accept Piaget's theory, his observations are indisputable, and have been replicated countless times. In my own research (Selley 1993) I have found that the next, and more stable, stage of understanding is to base predictions on the nature of the material that the object is made of. (This distinction between object and substance, and the concept 'being made of', are not found in very young children.) So wood, plastic etc. float while iron (and all metals), stone, and glass things sink. It is as if the materials know the right thing to do – they know their place, as Aristotle taught, 2,400 years ago.

However, this simple model is really no more than a classified list of materials: there isn't really any explanation in it. So when we ask, 'Why does wood, or cork, or foam-plastic float?' we are asking, 'What do all these floating substances have in common, that sinking substances don't have?' And the answer which comes up most frequently, around the age of six to sixty, is that they contain air. The evidence is quite firm: we can almost see the air pockets in cork or wood (cut across the grain); and cardboard, which floats at first, gradually gives out air bubbles, and sinks.

Likewise a sponge, if squeezed hard. A glass bottle, full of air, will float; while the same, filled with water, will sink.

So the 'air causes floating' model is a good one: it works, doesn't it? Well, no. There is a counter-example lurking not far out of sight: the candle. (I advise you to keep this hidden until the more straightforward objects have been tested and discussed.) The candle floats, although it visibly does not contain air (though I have known at least one child claim that the air in the hole down the middle must be responsible!). Some types of polythene also float, without air content; and of course oil (though this, being a liquid, does not seem to 'count' with some people). The air model has reached its limit, and must be replaced.

No satisfactory replacement will be available to the child until the arrival of the concept of density. Then we can say 'Things float if they are light for their size', i.e. of low density. (Why isn't there a word for this: undense?) At first the model is crude, for it does not specify how dense something must be in order to sink. But this model, unlike its predecessor, can grow. In secondary school pupils will meet the refinement that buoyancy depends on the relation between the density of the object and the density of the liquid it is immersed in. This in turn leads to many fascinating and amusing tricks – and serious matters such as the Gulf Stream (and our personal comfort).

Figure 7 Questions, embodying children's alternative conceptions, can be presented in cartoon form (see also Keogh and Naylor 1997).

What is a teacher of, say, Year 4 to do with some pupils who can readily use the air model to explain and predict, but who are perplexed by the candle? One solution is to do nothing, and let the children regard the candle wax as an oddity or anomaly. In an atmosphere of mutual trust, any child dissatisfied with this will come back and ask you again. Another way would be to talk about whether size has anything to do with floating, and to produce a block of wood and a stone weighing the same. (The children may or may not be impressed by this new angle.) In my opinion the worst thing to do would be to make the class copy into their science books some statement of the 'density' theory of buoyancy.

Mechanics

This is a branch of science which has given teachers an unnecessary amount of anxiety, because although the experiential base is very familiar, the experts' model, for analysing and explaining this experience, is erudite.

For example, take forces: pushes and pulls, so simple that we could easily teach this to KS1. I agree, as long as we keep to visible (by this I mean tangible) forces, such as prodding with a stick, or tugging by a string. These are forces which can have detectable effects, like causing a change in motion, or a dent or bend in a material. But in more advanced physics we soon come across mysterious forces due to gravity, or magnetism. Weight is the force of attraction between an object and the Earth, and since the Earth is so much heavier than the object, we ignore the effect on it, and regard weight as the pull of the Earth on our object. But in practice we only notice this weight when the situation is such that something is holding the object back from falling to Earth: such as when it is resting on a weak surface like clay, and is slowly sinking in; or hanging by a weak thread, near to breaking point. Then we can readily agree that weight is a force, because we have made it act on something else. It seems as if the weight is *in* the heavy object. (Try lifting a heavy suitcase: you can feel the weight of it, or in it.)

So far this is good material for primary school. But the experts who write the textbooks are not satisfied with this simple-minded version. They want to insist that weight is a force acting *on* the object all the time. Children aged 9, 11 and even 16 regularly show in tests that they do not recognize any force acting downwards on a ball in flight; the experts deplore this, and blame the teachers for not teaching them right.

Likewise for a teapot resting on a table. The beginner is tempted to show the weight force acting at the base of the teapot (where it presses down on the table); but the approved version of the theory has it that the force

of gravity acts on every part of the teapot, downwards (and seeming to act on a point at the centre, where – as we see if we take the lid off – there is nothing!). The force on the teapot base is upwards, not downwards (it is the weight reflected back, as it were, by the table). There have been exam questions and even KS2 SATs which have required children to show, by arrows, the forces acting within some system; and almost all candidates have got this wrong, unless they were willing to abandon common sense, and memorise the approved answers. I would call these questions inappropriate and unfair; others (especially the children?) might call them wicked.

It is for this reason that I have looked in some detail at the teaching of forces: to warn trainee teachers about the danger of trying to teach a theory which is much more advanced than your pupils can grasp. This advice may sound like holding the children back, but I would argue that it is shielding them from the lure of false knowledge. The constructivist approach is to work with the children, helping them to develop their own models. It is not good enough to teach them to give a superficial appearance of advanced knowledge.

Perhaps I might offer two maxims. Never try to teach anything that you don't understand yourself. And, if you do understand it, never try to teach *all* that you know.

Biology

At one time almost the only science taught in primary schools was nature study, and although there was a lot that was good in this, the approach came under attack for its lack of scientific method. True, there is not much you can do with flowers, seedlings, stick insects or toads, except to observe – and admire. Certainly any experimentation with the animals, even if it did them no harm, would not now be approved. Also, the identification of specimens by means of handbooks is of little value for its own sake.

To supply the scientific content that was felt to be lacking in nature study requires an appeal to theory and explanation. Some activities make use of chemical and physical theories to provide the causes for living processes such as movement (including in water and in the air), respiration, seed dispersal and digestion. But this type of theory is generally too advanced and unsuitable for KS1 or 2. Likewise, the great theories of biology – evolution, genetics, and disease – are not easy to simplify for young children.

The theories which I think are possibly the best candidates for underpinning the study of living things, at primary school level, are:

1. Adaptation or, to put it simply, the assumption that every part of a living organism has a function which is beneficial to it;

2. Life cycles (including sexual reproduction in vertebrates and flowering plants)[1];
3. Growth and nutrition (including food).

In most cases the starting point for the study will be the human being, and the children themselves will be objects for observation. Teeth, bones, joints, the senses, body measurements, temperature, breathing, diet, water intake and excretion can all be studied and discussed by use of the theories just mentioned.

It is worth remembering that the topics which people are most interested in are also those about which it is dangerous to be dogmatic. Advice on healthy diet and lifestyle is particularly susceptible to revision. The scientific approach of unemotional, open-minded scepticism is a useful counterweight against fads, myths, and moralistic pronouncements.

Growth

Growth is a fascinating topic, because it occurs too slowly to be directly observable. 'Watching the grass grow' is well known to be a leisurely activity. So, if animals and plants do not grow when we are watching them, when *do* they grow? It must be during the night, according to many children. (It is actually quite easy to set up a device which, by lever action, magnifies the growth of a bean plant so that the growth of a few millimetres per hour becomes detectable.)

A rather more difficult conception to challenge by observational evidence is the common confusion of growth with maturation, 'You'll understand all this when you're grown up' (or 'when you're bigger'). Children sometimes associate growth with age, and suppose that they grow substantially in the night before their birthdays, the date on which they 'become bigger'.

The mechanism of growth is worth discussion: a common model at Year 2–4 is that it is simply expansion, like a balloon being blown up, or a sponge swelling up in water. Some children think that we get bigger in order to make room for our food (rather like Christmas afternoon). Only later do children become capable of imagining growth as the addition of substance, of the same kind as that which is already there, and from the inside. The idea of food, whether fish, chips or rice, being transformed into various animal parts – arm muscles and bones, fingernails, cat's whiskers or whatever – is an idea which is so mysterious and wonderful that it has

---

1 I would include seed production and dispersal, but I have great reservations about the teaching of pollination as an analogy to fertilization by a male animal, since this is a formal analogy, not an observable one.

been remarked upon by poets, and deserves to be *taught* as being mysterious and wonderful.

Susan Carey (Carey 1985) interviewed children to find out their concept of 'alive', and found that they were frequently confused between alive as the opposite of dead, and live (living material), the opposite of inanimate. This should serve as a warning to teachers, that if they wish to discuss 'living things' with children, they should first establish a very clear and simple definition of what they are talking about. Students usually accept movement, eating and breathing as criteria for life, but they rarely include 'growth'.

Investigation

Science Attainment Target 1 (Sc1) was originally called exploration of science, and many would say that that was a more suitable name, for the primary school, than the revised title. For KS1 no-one would quarrel with the statement that:

> Pupils should observe familiar materials and events in their immediate environment, at first hand, using their senses; [and] describe and communicate their observations, ideally through talking in groups ...
>
> (DES 1989)

The latest (1995) document now calls this section experimental and investigative science, which to my ear sounds more teacher-directed; and the reference to talking in groups has gone, replaced by added emphasis on drawings and charts.

Nevertheless, it would be a mistake to try to 'save time' by cutting down on the talking part of science. Young children need the immediate confirmation or challenge that comes from verbal communication. As they try to make someone else see the curious, or perplexing, feature which they have observed, they are under pressure to make their meaning clear, and to check that it is a defensible interpretation. The teacher should be on hand frequently, for at least two reasons: she is able to provide a better-informed audience for the child's ideas; and she is likely to be quicker to pick up and acknowledge an unusual and original suggestion. But of course the teacher cannot be with every group all the time, so some strategy is required which will keep the children engaged on, and interested in, their discussion, unaided.

One way to do this is to arrange that the children's discussion results in some action: for instance, that they agree on some 'story' (account) of their exploration, to tell to the teacher eventually, or perhaps to the class ('show and tell'). A similar strategy is for the teacher to set in advance, perhaps in large print on a card, some questions on which the children must try to agree an answer.

Very rarely, at least below Year 5, should the children be expected to communicate their thoughts in writing. The process would be too slow, and the result would most likely be that any original and substantial thought about the science would be lost, and replaced by relatively trivial or routine accounts of apparatus and procedure. This is not to say that children should never be asked to describe their activity, or draw up a table of results; but these tasks will be for practice (i.e. instruction in the technique), and are unlikely to assist in the investigation itself, either the planning or the interpreting.

At KS2, children should be able to begin to plan their investigations. The first step is that they recognize and state what the question is that they are hoping to answer as the outcome of the investigation. An 'experiment' goes beyond an exploration, in that it has a more definite purpose than 'To see what happens if ...'. Time spent helping the pupils to explicitly formulate their questions is time well spent, because an investigator with a clear aim will be able to proceed far more independently than one who is not sure what he/she is supposed to be doing.

What to investigate

The choice of topic for investigation can cause the teacher a lot of worry, if the choice is constrained by incompatible requirements – and this has often been the case. I suggest that it is impossible to satisfy, in one and the same practical investigation, the following two criteria:

1. The investigation is to be planned, conducted and interpreted by the pupil; and
2. The outcome is to be knowledge and understanding of the topic, as intended by the teacher and required by the curriculum.

The teacher should avoid this trap by deciding, at the lesson planning stage, whether the practical activity is:

A. a true, open investigation, or
B. instruction in some practical techniques, or
C. a directed experience intended to further the pupil's knowledge and understanding, perhaps to illustrate a theory that has already been taught.

Each of these purposes will require a different role for the pupils and teacher, especially with regard to the amount of detail in the instructions, and the nature of the outcome. (A may have a 'conclusion', while for B the outcome might be 'I did it right', and for C 'It worked!')

The assessment of the skill or process of investigation is not easy to define, though it can be done by a teacher who is fully conversant with the scientific attitude. One feature which has received a lot of attention, due to its inclusion in the NC, is the fair test, and the whole business of variables. Unfortunately the prominence given to this feature of the so-called scientific method has led to some forced and artificial practice, and to the neglect of other, equally important skills.

Some (but by no means all) scientific investigations are best pursued by identifying in advance a pair of 'key variables'. These are observable, or measurable, features of the set-up, which are expected to affect one another in a definite way. The hypothesis is that if it is true that Q (length, size, motion, colour, or whatever) is caused by P (food supply, temperature, wetness, or height above the Earth), then if we change P (but nothing else) we should get a corresponding change in Q. The one we intend to change, P, may be called the experimental variable (because we are going to experiment with it); and Q is the dependent variable, because it is dependent on P[1].

So, one feature P is to be altered, and we shall watch to see how Q responds. But the result will only be meaningful if we can be sure that nothing else has been changed. It may be known, or suspected, or not yet realised, that a change in R also affects the value of Q: so it is important that R should not change during the experiment: R must thus be 'controlled' (i.e. kept constant), and so it is called a control variable. Only when all conceivable control variables have been thought of, and kept under control, do we have a fair test.

This may sound very technical (and perhaps it was meant to), but in practice the fair test is not difficult or unfamiliar to children, if they understand what is going on. It takes a very naive eight-year-old not to realise that if runners start from a 'straight' starting line on a curved track, the runner in the outside lane will be at a disadvantage.

An anecdote may help to illustrate the issue. Three pupils in Y6 were investigating the heat-conducting property of three spoons made of plastic, wood, and steel. They decided to use a stopwatch (a 'scientific instrument') to measure the time it took for the spoon handle to feel warm after the spoon was placed in hot water. Hot water from a kettle was placed in a

---

1 In advanced work P is called the independent variable, but I advise you never to use this unintelligible label. In graphs (not likely to be used below Y5) the experimental variable is displayed along the horizontal axis. The experimental and dependent variables, P and Q, can also be called the input and the output variables.

glass beaker, and the first pupil picked up the first spoon, put it in the water, and the second pupil started the watch. As soon as she felt the handle get warm she called, 'Stop', and the time (accurate to a second) was entered in the table of results by pupil 3. Then pupil 1 picked up the next spoon (wood), and put it into the hot water. This time the time which elapsed was much greater. Then the third (metal) spoon was tested, in the same hot (by now warm) water – and came out as the worst conductor. We may safely say that concentration on 'accuracy' had made this group oblivious to the far more important need to control the initial temperature by replacing the hot water each time.

Some primary children can appreciate the fair test, as is shown by the child's reply to the question as to why she had put equal volumes of hot water in the jars in a 'cooling' experiment: 'To be fair'. On being pressed, she explained, 'If it takes longer to boil a larger amount of water, therefore it would take a larger amount of water longer to cool down'.

However, it is easy to be wise after the event, and asking children to state in their Plans what they intend to keep the same (such a common feature of Planning Sheets now) is not always successful. If we could anticipate all difficulties when planning (journeys, moving house, school trips!) life would be unexciting. Pupils are far more likely to notice an overlooked control variable while the experiment is underway if they are alert. It is true that then they will have to start again, having wasted time, but they will be the wiser for it. Fair testing is a way of working, an attitude to the meaning of evidence, and an appreciation of the meaning of validity[1].

It is not a simple skill which can be reduced to a few rules, or taught in a few lessons. Even professional scientists sometimes lapse, to their subsequent embarrassment, and the glee of their rivals.

I would stress that an intelligent, alert attitude to the quality of the investigation can only be arrived at by a pupil who has accepted responsibility for it. The student must know what the question is, must want to find a solution, must know of a promising line of procedure, must know how to set up and manipulate the necessary apparatus ... and must expect to be allowed to extract the meaning from the results.

---

1 The apparent simplicity of the term 'fair test' has led teachers to ask children, engaged on an investigation, questions such as, 'What must you do to make it fair?' This can be confusing, in that the word has a moral connotation of equity, or equal opportunities. To some Year 2 children, who were being led through an investigation into the best growth conditions for beans, the whole idea of depriving one specimen of water (to show that water was necessary) was unfair, because it might hurt the plant. To many adults, too, it is regarded as unfair that in clinical drugs trials, one group of sufferers (the control group) has the curative treatment deliberately withheld, and usually without being told so.

My point is that, despite its apparent familiarity, the term 'fair test' is a technical term, and should be taught only when the teacher is satisfied that the pupils are ready for it.

These conditions are not likely to be satisfied by an 'investigation' thought up by a teacher (or author), and conveyed through precise instructions. Nor will the final requirement (freedom of interpretation) be possible if the teacher already knows what result to expect, and intends to ensure that it is reached.

I believe that a successful investigation is only possible if the topic (problem) is an *unimportant* one, in the sense that whatever the outcome, it can be accepted without causing conflict with the content syllabus for the immediate future. This cannot be emphasised enough.

On this principle it would be unsuitable to suggest or promote, as a Year 6 or 7 investigation, the measurement of the boiling point of water, or the question, 'Does oil mix with water?', because 'wrong' answers would be an embarrassment. Likewise, 'How much does a spring (or elastic band) stretch with various loads?' does not really allow alternative results, and the emphasis is likely to be on getting the approved results, rather than on ingenuity in planning. Activities like these have their value, but they are Type B or C in the list given at the start of this section.

In contrast, some questions for true investigation might include:

1. Compare the quality of some year-old elastic bands with some new ones;
2. Somebody has heard that putting moist salt on grass stains before washing helps to get them out. Try it.
3. Which kind of string or thread makes the best 'string telephone'?
4. Birds on the ground (perhaps feeding) usually fly away when approached. Are they alerted by the sight of movement, or the sound, or the smell of the approaching animal (e.g. us)?
5. How strong (or close) does a magnet have to be, to distort the music on a cassette tape? (Use pin-lifting as a magnetic field measure?) Don't let them try this on your bank card!

You may have noticed that some of these investigations tend towards the 'technology' style, of 'making it work'. There is an affinity with 'problem solving' activities which were very popular a few years ago (e.g., build the highest tower out of five sheets of A4 paper); but I think that the science investigations place more emphasis on understanding some specific theory, rather than general 'know-how' of mechanical construction. But one sort can often unexpectedly turn into the other; and both are valuable in their own way.

The constructivist approach here is that people learn to investigate, not by being told how, but by trying out their own ideas. The teacher, as a patient listener, can often steer the child away from time-consuming disasters, by asking supplementary questions; but not to the extent of taking charge. The greatest challenge is likely to come from children who have been socialised, perhaps at home, into an attitude of deference to adults which paralyses them from proposing any plan of action for themselves. They may say that they don't know what to do, whereas they may actually mean that they daren't suggest anything. At present I have no solution to offer.

There may also be a gender or class issue at play, as with the Year 5 boys who declined to investigate leaves, giving as the reason, 'We don't do trees'. The same might apply to clothes, machines, batteries, and washing powders. How to respond? Give free choice of topic (and perpetuate the discrimination)? Or set the topic, and then coax and challenge, with emphasis on the methodology? Perhaps we should take seriously the recent DfEE exhortation, in Circular 4/98 p. 71, about: 'engaging *all* pupils' interest in science' (my emphasis) including 'helping pupils to realise the contribution of different civilisations to our knowledge in science'. This will necessitate links with history and geography, and a consideration of the effects of science on culture, which can only be to the benefit of all pupils. Topics such as 'houses and homes', 'travel and navigation', 'agriculture and food' and 'medicines and drugs' are all rich opportunities for cross-curricular integration.

CHAPTER 7

Language

Writing

The use of the constructivist approach to teaching language is rarely discussed, possibly because language and communication seem such obviously personal processes. We might assume that speaking and listening are always in touch with what the child already knows, and that creative writing gives sufficient opportunity for self-expression.

However, this may be something of an illusion. In some classrooms the teaching of language may incorporate many constraints and prescriptions, arising from the teacher's anxiety that the child should attain competence in standard English and to make progress towards assessable competences. This can result in failure to appreciate and praise individual achievement if it is less impressive than the norm.

A common example of this is the quandary of how to respond to a child's first attempts at extended writing. The piece may be almost indecipherable, with almost every word mis-spelt, but as a step towards written communication it may be a significant advance. Marian Sainsbury (1996:52) has provided us with a copy of the first full-length (two page) story that a Year 1 girl had ever written. The lexicography is idiosyncratic, but it succeeds, in that the child-author was able to read the whole piece back. The constructivist teacher might well decide that, for the moment, this function as personal record and aide-mémoire should be regarded as sufficient, and so no 'corrections' should be made or even thought of. The 'significant achievement' here is the girl's realisation that she can capture an extended narrative by encoding it on paper.

It is widely recognised that most children want to write because they see the value of being able to transmit messages to other people (e.g. by sending or leaving notes), or recording ideas for future retrieval, or some other 'human sense' reason. They can be highly motivated by this, and will spend long periods engaged on tasks of this kind. But they are not usually motivated by any desire merely to generate technically correct sentences. This is more likely to be the teacher's obsession than theirs.

The constructivist strategy, then, would be to try to provide a purpose (and hence a desire) for writing activities. This would include a plausible recipient of the proposed piece (i.e. not the teacher alone), a real or contrived context for it, and something to say (this might be reached through talk, as a preliminary stage); and not least, some opportunity for originality, humour or wit.

In order to endorse the view that writing is primarily for communication, the teacher might sometimes refrain from 'corrections' entirely, and instead provoke some response by remarks, questions or objections to the content of the piece, rather than to its presentation.

A similar dilemma arises regarding the provision of 'good models' of writing for children to follow. If these are not close to writings which the child would have chosen, they may simply oppress, and become either an unhelpful or an unattainable target. It is of course important that each pupil should have access to, and some familiarity with, a range of written styles. But it could be counter-productive to insist that these should be imitated.

On the other hand, there are cases of children being inspired to create endless stories in the genre of their favourite published stories; the salient point being that these were chosen and adopted by the children themselves. In the happy phrase of Nigel Hall (1989:x), it is 'authorship' that we should be helping young children to develop. In his book there are reports of how this was approached through letter writing (children to each other, and to the teacher 'as a person'), and imaginative stories inspired by an unusual object (in fact, a one-eyed toy monkey).

Finally, let us examine the device, so common in primary schools, of separating creative writing from English exercises. The purpose may be an admirable one, namely the removal of the need to mar 'compositions' with intrusive technical corrections, on the grounds that these are being dealt with through the drill exercises. But in a devastating critique, Myra Barrs (in Mills and Timson 1988:82) quotes the Bullock report: 'Explicit instruction out of context is in our view of little value', and then discusses why this routine of grammar teaching, exercises and drills is such an extraordinarily inefficient way of teaching language. She concludes that:

> Perfectly adapted to the acquisition of language in real human contexts, and to the use of a complex grammar that is inductively and unconsciously acquired, [the human mind] proves stubbornly intractable to attempts to teach language through deductive methods which require the conscious application of grammatical principles.

After pointing out the artificiality and frequent insensitivity of drill books, she reminds us that the hours spent on practising commas, apostrophes and doubled letters may have no effect or even the opposite effect on the learner from that intended:

> With a kind of mad solicitude, the writers of these books continually point out to the children the very connections that they want them to ignore ... Off and of, here and hear, ... to, too and two are practised until it is a wonder that there (their, they're) is a child in the land who doesn't confuse them.

If this analysis is correct, and it is the case that the errors which so many adults make were actually taught to them at school, then we must seriously consider new ways of getting back to basics, in the sense of teaching children to achieve technical competence in written English. The most promising direction, it seems to me, is to anchor children's writing in what they are able to do, that is, to speak fluently. Gradually, as they read, they will notice discrepancies with the words they write, and will be impelled to resolve those discrepancies. The teacher can perhaps help by drawing the child's attention to (but not correcting) some such cases. It is a long-term job, and will have to continue into the secondary school (where the staff will have to take on the responsibility). It would also seem to be a mistake to teach punctuation too soon. Young children often do not speak in well-formed, complex sentences, and the pauses in their speech do not serve as reliable indicators for the placement of commas (which are there to aid semantic decoding, not elocution). Perhaps the whole business should be postponed until Key Stage 2, after the children have got the words right. It would be a pity if compliance with the Literacy Hour were to preclude experimentation in this area.

The other firm basis for language learning is the child's world of experience and meaning. If the child's writing draws upon that knowledge (rather than being driven by meaningless grammar or comprehension exercises), there is some chance that the desire to communicate truthfully and successfully will provide the motivation for technical improvement. We are all in favour of teaching language skills – who isn't? – and the only dispute is about the analysis of the source of the problem, and the consequent pedagogy.

Reading and speaking

The reading of literature is an interactive process. At one level, the interaction is one of motivation: the reader will not concentrate on the words unless there is some expectation of reward such as enjoyment or usefulness. At a more elevated and intangible level, every reader (or listener, for that matter) plays a part in the semantic transaction, and helps to create some meaning out of those words.

Literature may arouse feelings, or provoke reflection or opposition. A good teacher-reader can sometimes grip and enthral all or most of her child-audience for a while, but it is surely impossible to arouse all of them all the time. Children have differing tastes, moods, and needs, so they must be allowed to choose what to read.

The question then arises: to what extent should the teacher, or school, exercise control over the 'quality' of literature provided? Teachers have, of course, an obligation to make available the best children's literature, and they can follow the press reviews, or consult a librarian, to keep up to date on that. But children seem to be perverse in their preferences. Linnea Timson ('A living through', in Mills and Timson 1988) describes how one child found personal meaning in a 'sentimental and badly illustrated book', while her own class enthusiastically devoured and discussed the Dr Seuss books which she had nearly discarded as 'not providing an appropriate literary experience for infants'.

Perhaps the resolution of this dilemma will come out of two-way trust: the teacher will offer the children the opportunity to read her/his preferred selection, trusting them to consider them adequately, though without obligation; the children will trust the teacher to recommend only those books which stand some chance of being recognised as significant by those children to whom they are proffered. I admit that this sounds rather a mature relationship, and out of line with current official recommendations.

Now I turn to the issue of the children's interpretation of what they read. The strong constructivist view is that meaning is constructed by the reader, and so, up to that point, the text has no meaning other than that which the reader has given it. The study of this process is known as hermeneutics. So it is not easy to find out whether the pupils have 'understood' any piece of text, for they will naturally suppose that they *have* (unless of course they found it totally incomprehensible). Whether their understanding of it is the same as the teacher's (let alone the author's) could only be researched through quite lengthy interviews or conversations. Only in the case of the most straightforward, uncomplicated, and hence boring texts can comprehension be tested by a short written test. 'How did the farmer get his cows to market? Why did he think that he had got a bargain?' The trouble is that to probe into the more subtle meanings which may lie hidden in a story or poem is a bit like asking someone to explain a joke: to expose is to diminish.

Despite the claim that the meaning is what the reader understands it to mean, it would probably be worthwhile, at Key Stage 2 or above, to lead pupils towards examining their own degree of certainty in their own interpretations. One way of doing this might be to invite the pupils to underline in colour anything they feel unsure of. Can they 'follow the plot'? And will other children agree with their version of it?

Children as critics

It is important that students of all ages should be allowed, indeed required, to generate their own reasoned opinions of literature (fiction and poetry), and not just to adopt and reproduce opinions which they have read or been told. The National Literacy Strategy, in the text-level strand, has some ambitious proposals for developing children's critical skills. For example, in Year 2 term 3, children will compare books, either by the same author or by different authors on the same theme, and form preferences, giving reasons. In Year 3 term 3 they will 'consider credibility of events' by comparing fictional and real-life accounts.

When they are allowed to be, even young children are literary critics. They will spontaneously come out with an appraisal of, say, a television drama. After showing a video of a children's drama, one Year 2 teacher asked the children to discuss which of the characters they had liked. After two or three contributions had been made, a girl surprised the group by saying that the one she liked best was the character called Marjorie, an aloof and supercilious girl who used her skill and cunning to turn events to her own advantage. 'I don't mean that I *like* her', the child explained, 'but I think she acted the part very well.'

This distinction, between empathy (for the 'good' characters) and critical approval of the actor's (and author's) representation, is one which I suppose we would wish to encourage. Yet it cannot be forced. Some six-year-olds would still refuse to admit that a 'bad' character could be approved of in any way at all. So the concept in question must be constructed by the child, not by the teacher – who can only provide the likely opportunity and then reinforce the outcome.

In a chapter 'Authors review authors' (Hall 1989), Susan Williams describes and illustrates how a group of five-year-olds wrote book reviews, and grew more critical, and more ready to form and express opinions. For example:

'All of the stories were good. But one of the stories was sad.'

'I don't like this book. It's horrible and nasty ... because Daddy Bear doesn't get any sleep.'

If we now look at a different aspect of children's understanding of texts, it seems that one source of imperfect communication is lack of skill in the use of qualifying conjunctions (if, but, although, as a result, etc.). These meanings have to be constructed by the child, as best he can, from the context. Any teacher wishing to help accelerate this process would be well advised to listen very carefully to each child's contributions to a (probably group) discussion. Well chosen questions may help to promote the use of more complex constructions in speaking: 'What would you have expected him to do?' 'How did she know that that was likely to happen?' (This language may of course need to be simplified.)

In the story of the *Three Billy-Goats Gruff*, the first goat advises the nasty Troll to spare him, and to wait for the next goat, his brother, who (he claims) will be found to be fatter. Besides raising interesting questions of ethics (since the first goat makes no move to warn his unsuspecting brother), this discussion provides admirable opportunities for practice in syntax, such as finding the right words to express a complicated thought. Was the first goat to be admired for cleverly escaping injury at the hands of the Troll? Or condemned for putting his brothers in danger? (The same dilemma arises repeatedly in fiction, whenever a deception is perpetrated. Every prisoner or spy who escapes through disguise as a nun or a nurse puts genuine nuns and nurses at greater risk.)

The principle behind these examples is a general one: that a child will make the effort to find the right means of expression, if and when he/she has something to say, and a desire to communicate it. The Literacy Hour now provides an opportunity for extended group and teacher discussion of deep questions, notionally uninterrupted by the rest of the class, for twenty minutes per week (per group). This unprecedented organisational change to regular sessions with groups of manageable size may enable teachers to achieve what many had previously found almost impossible to provide, namely a rich and liberating educational experience of literature.

CHAPTER 8

History

Compared to some other curriculum areas, there has been little research into children's ideas in history. Consequently there is little to inform the teacher of specific cases of children constructing historical concepts, nor specific programmes which show cognitive progression.

However, much can be done by applying the general principles of the constructivist approach, starting with the challenge of helping children to construct a sense of past time, through to an awareness of the provisional character of all historical narratives, together with some skill (almost a knack) of judging the plausibility of a story by appraising the evidence for and against it.

In this short chapter I shall look first at the way this approach can influence the teaching of the conceptual bases of history to very young children. Then we shall jump to the upper primary years, to see how capable children are of reasoning about history (i.e. using meta-concepts such as causality and evidence). Finally I shall take a quick look at the influence of postmodernism, and the liberating (or perhaps worrying) suggestion that there is, in any case, no historical truth to be found.

Young children's sense of the past

The first conceptual areas to be tackled are likely to be: (1) building a sense of time extending back into the past; and (2) a comparison between ordinary life in the distant past, and today's experiences. This will lead to the concept of historical change, and rate of change.

Children can recover, from their own memories, some personal recollections of events (birthdays, holidays etc.), and phases of life such as a previous class or playgroup. They can try to place these in chronological order – probably in reverse. Then they may be reminded of more public knowledge, known to many children in the class; photographs may help here. The teaching objective is to help the child to construct a sense of time, extending over months or years, and to recognise that this time-scale can also be tied in with those originated by other children.

Of course there will be a temptation for the teacher to map these time-lines on to the calendar, but this should not be over-emphasised. At first the sequence, and the feeling for the stretching-back of time, should be allowed to grow through the fitting-together of memories. 'A long time ago', 'not very long' and 'yesterday' need to be well grounded before a child can put dates to them. Sequencing is a skill of which the young child is justifiably proud (and which is evident in the continuous chains of 'and then we ... (did this) and then we (went there) ...' in their narratives.

Following this, we can move back to family history dating back 10 to 50 years: parents' and grandparents' life-stories, photographs of older siblings looking young, old furniture (not necessarily in the derogatory sense) still in use at home or at school; and old buildings. Questions such as, 'Which of these looks older?' can focus attention on salient clues. Old domestic artefacts, from toasting-fork to the all-metal tricycle or washbowl, can help to give substance to the sense of the past.

I hold to the theory that, at first, there is no continuity between a child's personal past and the long-ago 'historical past', as seen on TV. Robin Hood, Queen Elizabeth I, cave-dwellers, Romans and the American Wild West are all 'elsewhere' in time and place. They represent story settings that are part fact, part fiction. Teachers find it difficult to get children to distinguish between history and myth, between Columbus and Jack (the one with the beanstalk), let alone Moses and the bulrushes. The constructivist advice would be not to push this too soon, but to listen to the individual child's comments and questions, and be ready to help when needed.

By Year 3, most children should possess a firm model for the recent past, calibrated either in terms of generations 'when my granny was a girl' or in decades (30 years ago). It comes naturally to adults in Europe to date things according to the two World Wars, but young children have so little direct contact with these events that they may not serve as good landmarks (time-marks) any more. To help to consolidate and elaborate these time-lines, the teacher will usually provide a large paper chart, or even a washing-line with objects and pictures hung on it. The more the children can partake in the construction of these, the better. If they are then given further items – either artefacts or pictures – to hang on the line, the outcome of their delib-erations should be respected. The timid teacher, who feels embarrassed at having, say, a picture of an old-style television hanging up at AD 1900, can label it as the children's estimate: 'We thought this looked as if ...' (the same could apply to a chandelier manufactured *circa* 1990).

It is important to present the task of observing and inferring in such a way as to value the children's ideas, and not to tempt them to guess at the answer an expert (e.g. the teacher) would give. With this in mind, Mary Aris (1993:60) gives a list of suggestions for 'questioning objects'. Children are asked, as they examine the object, 'What is it like?' (feel like, smell like, made of, complete or broken); then, 'How do you think it was made?' (what from, by hand or machine, from bits fixed together?) and 'What do you think it was made for?' She advises against the questions, 'What is it?' and, 'What date?', because children may think that as soon as they have guessed these answers they have finished, and will move on to the next item, as in a quiz game. Naturally, if the children see evidence which points towards this information they will say so, without having to be asked.

We should never miss the opportunity, however, to ask children to comment on how sure they are of their suggestions (such as what an artefact was made of, or for). The appreciation of the process – of inference from evidence (i.e. clues) to other information – is a vital part of school history (Smith and Holden 1994).

Children's appreciation of the concept of historical explanation

Children can make a start at acquiring the concepts of historical time at an early age, probably within Key Stage 1. But 'explanation' is definitely more advanced.

Peter Lee and colleagues (Lee *et al.* 1996:6–11) studied the progression of children's understanding of explanation, and the meaning of the word 'because', at Key Stages 2 and 3. One small part of their research was an investigation into whether children recognise any difference between giving information, and presenting that same information as an explanation.

The Romans took over Britain. The Roman army had good weapons.

The Romans were able to take over Britain because their army had good weapons.

Is there any real difference between these boxes, or do they say the same thing really? Explain why you think yes or no.

Very few of the Y3 and Y6 children (15 and 20%) could see any difference. A Y6 boy wrote: 'I think no because both of them mean that the Romans took over and had good weapons.' But at least one Y3 girl knew an explanation when she saw one: 'Box 1 is not explaining that the Roman army won because of its weapons. Box 2 is.'

By Y7 50% of the children thought there was a difference, and most of these mentioned that Box 2 was an explanation. Some even made the quite sophisticated point that even if Box 1 were true, Box 2 might be false, because there could be other reasons. Steven (Y7) wrote:

> I think there is a real difference because Box 1 is stating pure facts and Box 2 is stating that the Romans won because they had good weapons, which they do not know. It may have been because they worked as a team.

It might seem odd that so many of the children fail to attach importance to the word 'because'. It cannot be that they don't know how to use it, because even the Y3 children were mostly able to create 'this because that' sentences in the context of their own actions, and often wrote responses beginning 'I think this because ...'. It seems that it is the concept of explanation *in history* which they lack. Lee *et al.* (1996:10) suggest that since a prime concern in history is the veracity of the facts, this can divert attention from the validity of the argument which is based upon them. In primary school history the principal intellectual task is to consider whether the descriptions of situations are plausible, and supported by evidence. From this angle, both boxes have the same content. Some children thought that the difference was merely one of style: that Box 2 put it all in one sentence 'to make it sound better'.

It strikes me as significant that children aged 8–14 have been found to have a similar difficulty in science, where they often fail to distinguish between the factual truth of a statement, and its function as a causal factor in the proposed explanation. (It is likely that jurors in court sometimes make the same mistake.) This points to the importance of providing tasks which encourage every pupil to engage in discussion about explanations, including some which may be faulty.

Teaching historical explanation

We must remember that the process of explaining means that the pupil must invent or at least adopt an explanation for some historical event, and be prepared to argue for it. This is completely different from having knowledge of an explanation (as devised by the experts), even if accompanied by knowledge of the evidence in favour of it.

Peter Knight has proposed (and trialled) an 'Explanations approach', in which the teacher not only provides information, but presses the pupils to answer 'Why?' While this was ineffective with infants, it had a measurable beneficial effect on learning at KS2 (see Aris 1993:41).

The constructivist approach would be to start with some well-known local event for which no explanation has yet been fully accepted; in other words, a mystery. The facts can be gleaned from local newspapers or radio, and the class then works in groups to decide on the most likely explanation. As a follow-up the children could be asked to consider whether their explanations invoke happenings which are speculative (i.e. which could perhaps be factually untrue), or whether the facts they cite are true but not necessarily adequate as explanations.

If you decide to use a fictionalised source, that is, a historical mystery story, you have entered the exotic border zone between history and literature. We find that theories abound – including ordinary human nature (greed and envy) psychology, or far-fetched conspiracy theories – which people get excited about. Some authors have made a fortune from books and films of this kind, so there must be something which fascinates people, and which we teachers could exploit.

It must be the case, logically, that every explanation is based upon some theory or other, even though these may not be stated explicitly. Hence there are various broad assumptions about the causes of events, which help us to make sense of the story. In literature about the past we find a number of such theories, which can be completely at odds with each other. For example:

- the 'destiny' theory of epics, legends and Greek tragedies;
- the 'technical superiority' theory as found in the Romans example above, and in most accounts of colonisation;
- the 'moral superiority' theory beneath stories of saints and heroes (and most war stories);
- the 'personal genius' theory used to account for leaders, discoverers, and industrialists.

It may help to make my point if I cite an example of a theory which was once popular in some societies, but has now fallen out of favour:

- the socialist or Marxist-Leninist theory of class struggle, and the ultimate victory of the proletariat.

(We will of course reject, for the purpose of teaching history, stories based on the sentimental theory of the ultimate victory of true love! The same presumably goes for racist (nationalist) explanations.)

I do not quite know what to say about one final theory of history, that events occur without real cause other than coincidence. It may often be true – but how boring!

Postmodernism

Children (and other humans) may ask, 'Did that really happen?', and put us in a quandary. We are aware that there can be no certainty when it comes to describing the past. What historians deal with are constructed histories, each with its own selection of so-called evidence to support its claims. My favourite statement of the postmodernist position pulls no punches (Appleby 1994): 'The full unknowability of the past event becomes the only real thing, in contrast to which the imaginative effort to reassemble a picture of past reality ... appears pathetic.'

Foucault and his followers have shown us how everyone reads into a text, or a narrative, the meaning which that reader prefers (and this can include an interpretation which he/she intends to reject, in which case she/he will tend to exaggerate the untenability of it). This has led some to the gloomy view that, since we can never know the past as it 'really' was, there is no point trying to narrate, let alone understand, it. There is no possibility of learning anything from history.

Other people (myself included) try to take a less extreme viewpoint. We accept that we have no direct access to knowledge of the external (objective) world of time and space. But the combined efforts of people in our culture have led to constructed accounts (or models) which, while never perfect, are moderately trustworthy. So it is worthwhile examining accounts for possible bias, possible errors and inconsistencies, and possible lessons for the future.

Since there cannot be one true (i.e. absolutely and indisputably true) history, we must be ready to consider and compare the versions on offer, knowing them all to be imperfect (Murphy 1996). Even if, in the absolute sense, none of the stories is 'true', they are not equally wrong. We must be critical, and alert.

Obviously a good time to learn to be critical and alert is at school, and the material for criticism could well be our own childish attempts to put together a self-consistent and illuminative account of certain events: in other words, to tell or write a true story (i.e. as true as can be). Children must be given the chance to comment on, correct, and suggest improvement to each other's efforts. They must also be encouraged to defend, amend and hold to their own stories – but not only because they are their own. They should come to value shared truth above idiosyncratic truth.

In classroom terms, each child should not only be able to put together a plausible story, but also be willing to listen patiently to others, and to be generous enough to accept any good ideas, yet confident enough to challenge faults. Obviously only a few children will be able to play a prominent role on any one day, so it will be a test of the teacher's record-keeping and management skills to ensure that all children get their turn eventually.

Creative and critical skills cannot be exercised without relevant knowledge, so it should go without saying that a substantial proportion of history lessons will be devoted to familiarisation with information, both fact and commentary; and both by teacher-telling and by book research.

CHAPTER 9
Mathematics

When I was about eight, my maternal grandmother, an unsophisticated countrywoman, put to me a riddle that clearly amused her, and which so impressed me that I have remembered it ever since:
  'How many beans make five?'
to which the answer was:
  'Four and a little one.'

We often treat the operation of counting as unproblematic, and assume that if carried out competently it will yield a unique result. It is rarely mentioned to children that a decision may have to be made as to what to include in the count. But it may matter greatly, for example if the objects are to be distributed as gifts. How many items are there in a set comprising a football, a pair of nail scissors, a fashionable pop CD, and a matchstick (quite apart from how many scissors there are in a pair)?

For some purposes we count *units*, rather than items. Three biscuits remain three even if one has broken (otherwise, in counting pieces of cake, we would have to count in each of the crumbs). The rule is: pieces which are fractions of a unit are not to be counted in with the 'wholes' (unless they can be aggregated to constitute a whole unit). Since this is rarely made explicit, children have to catch on to the convention by trial and error. The children who, when asked to divide ten biscuits between three, arrived at the 'mistaken' answer 'four each' had not recognised this (see Figure 8).

Of course there are many ill-defined concepts in common use (e.g. road/street, soap/detergent, pipe/tube, old/mature), and we have little difficulty with them. The distinctions usually don't matter, and when they do, we take extra care. But the trouble with mathematics is that it has the reputation for being exact and unambiguous; so teachers find themselves treating any but the correct meaning as a mistake.

Mathematics is perhaps the most unlikely school subject to be seen as needing a constructivist approach. There seems little to be gained by trying

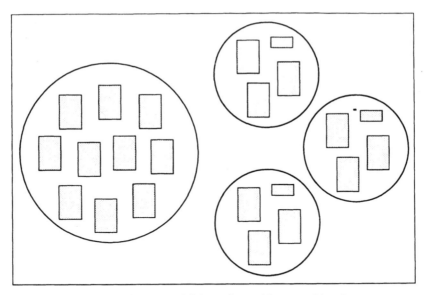

Figure 8 Some children showed how ten biscuits
shared between three people gave four each.

to find out a child's ideas, let alone to engage with them, if they are wrong. The teacher's traditional role is to show the correct method, set practice exercises, detect mistakes and correct them.

The case against this pedagogy is that it seems to have led to thousands of people who have left school with a dislike of mathematics, and no confidence in their ability to calculate anything. The attitude that there is one correct set of operations and that all others are wrong inevitably leads to many pupils being shown up as failing. Worse than that, they are forced to accept that they are unintelligent and irrational, for they cannot comprehend why their attempts are unsuccessful.

Some success has been claimed for the constructivist approach, which allows the teacher to work alongside the pupil on a task, and to listen to the reasoning behind each step. The assumption is that when a person is working on a problem, even if they do not seem to be succeeding, they have some reason for each move they make. This is quite different from the robot-like process of following an algorithm, or rote-learned procedure. It is even more different from the random guessing characteristic of the pupil who is in a blind panic, torn between anxiety and guilt.

Constructivism may involve the pupil in practical activity, but it may at other times involve listening intently to the teacher. It may well involve talking with other children, engaged on a shared task. Andrew Davis (Davis and Pettitt 1994:17), in support of a constructivist teaching style, states that, 'to encourage interactive working and discussions of certain kinds is likely to foster the growth of a greater number and range of connections between mathematical elements than an unrelieved diet of solitary study'.

It would obviously help a child to understand his/her own methods, meanings, assumptions and aims, by talking the task through with an attentive teacher. But of course, with a large class there is not going to be much chance of this: 39 into one won't go! What are the alternatives?

1. Group work, on a common task

Children have to talk to each other, explain what they think they should try, and why. Anyone who does not see the point will ask for it to be explained more clearly. As the discussion is between peers, there should be less inhibition due to deference. Objections will be raised, perhaps over matters of fact (e.g. the units of measurement) or of interpretation ('that's not what we were asked to do'). The task can be either a well-defined exercise (of a kind that at least some will remember from the past), or a more open investigation. The teacher may be appealed to to resolve disagreements.

Note that group work has many benefits as a teaching method, quite apart from management concerns such as the pupil:teacher ratio. It should be collaborative work, however, and not just children sitting in groups but working alone. For this collaboration to occur, the children must be able to trust you, the teacher, to accept the outcome of the group's deliberations, and not to insist that only your own (and as yet undisclosed) method is right. If the children perceive ambiguity and risk in the situation they may be averse to group work, but, as Gipps (1992: 21) tells us, 'when cooperative group work is facilitated, there are high levels of task-related talk' and 'interactions tend to be higher-order rather than routine'.

2. Mathematical investigations

Perhaps the distinctive feature of investigations is that the method is not prescribed, and may even not have been taught before at all. Each pupil makes up and tries out their individual method, which, we must accept, will often be less elegant than one that the expert might know. But, whether clumsy, long-winded, or incomplete, it is an achievement, and will gain credit as such[1].

---

1 One of my favourite resources for investigations is a bag of about a hundred 2p coins (they are surprisingly cheap!).
Problem (a): given ten coins, find out how many could be laid out to cover the table.
Problem (b): starting with a base row of four, build a triangle. How many moves (of one coin to any new position) are required to invert the triangle? Then try larger triangles. Is there a pattern to the results? (Two Year 4 pupils solved all the triangles from four to ten along the base, and drew a diagram showing every move in detail. There are two rules, one for even-numbered bases and one for odd.)

3. Trying to find different ways to do a problem

When they have finished, children compare their methods, and if they differ, try to see how the alternative worked. (More advanced pupils might make an appraisal.) If the methods are the same, they join up with another pair, until they find a variant. Even adults like to choose their own methods. When, recently, I asked 25 non-specialist teachers-in-training to add 8+5+7+5 (listed vertically), they used various methods, such as (5+5=10) (8+7=8×2–1); or 2×(7+5)+1. None added the numbers sequentially.

4. Writing instructions or exercises

Children who think they have solved a problem have to record their method in some way. Another child then tries to follow this 'recipe', applying it to a new problem – watched by the originator. Alternatively, children who feel confident with a mathematical technique go on to invent their own exercises in it. As an extension, they try to push the technique on to untried examples. When they find something new, they tell their teacher, who may designate a group of other pupils for the discoverer to show it to.

5. Multiple solutions

To help shake the assumption that there is always one right answer, set some exercises which have several valid solutions, mixed in with univalent ones (unique solutions). In both cases, after the first correct answer, ask 'Does anyone have another answer?'

Examples
a) What two-digit number, when reversed, becomes smaller by nine?
b) Tom has twin sisters, and each child has a party on their (his/her) birthday. How many parties per year? Answer: two (obviously), or one (if Tom's birthday is on the same day as his sisters'); or three (!).

6. Number stories

The children read, or are told, a fictional story which incorporates some calculations or mathematical reasoning as part of the plot. Afterwards they have to remember, or write down, what the number plot was, and to comment on it. Did they agree? Could they have done it a better way? (The pupils are not expected to remember the actual figures: these could be written on a poster etc.)

A nice easy number poem is *Five Eyes* by Walter de la Mare; the solution is only revealed in the last line.

Children's difficulties with numerals

Recent research, e.g. by Hughes (1986) and Labinowicz (1985), has shown that two features of traditional school mathematics give rise to difficulties and unnecessary stress. One is the premature move to the use of abstract numbers as objects in themselves. The other is premature training in the symbols and conventional display of arithmetical computations in isolation from meaningful situations involving numeracy. I think that these should now be illustrated in turn.

The question, 'What's two and two?' is a bit weird, on first encounter. (Answer: 'a pair of numbers'?) Perhaps it is a shortened form of, 'What is the sum of two and two?' or, 'What is the result of adding two and two together?' To the young child, the important missing information is still: two *what*?

By reception class, most children know that two bricks put in with two more bricks makes a group of four bricks. Soon after, they are comfortable with the computation that three cakes added to five cakes makes eight cakes altogether. But they cannot make any 'human sense' of the statement that three and five make eight. Either the statement is just deficient, in that the nouns are missing. Or, if you mean the symbols '3' and '5', it is simply false to say that you can group them in any way that looks like '8'.

The cardinal numbers can be used to describe something about a set: three cakes, for example, just as you might have 'hot cakes'. But it would be illogical (a category error) to try to add 'hot' and 'round', unless cakes were also mentioned. ('What's hot and round?' sounds like a feeble attempt at a riddle.) There is a long way to go, requiring recognition of the similarity between additions and subtractions of various concrete objects, before the numbers come to mean the general label for *any* set containing that many members.

Probably a useful move towards generalised arithmetic is tallying. Representing three cakes firstly by a drawing of three cakes, then three strokes \\\, then on to three dots :.

The question, 'What is 3 dots added to 5 dots?' (answer '8 dots') is getting fairly close to 3+5. Then: 'What would be 5 dots and 3 more?' ('dots' implied but unspoken) is even closer. But the decision to take the leap into zero-dimensional space, where numbers exist without material referents, can only be taken by the learner, voluntarily. (It is said to help, if the child makes invisible dots, by touching the table with her finger. The resulting 8 ghost dots can then be banished, leaving only the 8.)

As we all know, millions of children have been taught to 'do their sums', and most eventually responded to training in formulations such as '3+5=8'. The trouble is that this skill is compartmentalised as completely different from the arithmetical procedure that it is supposed to symbolise. Children aged about six, even if they are accustomed to written arithmetic, do not choose these formulations as a means of recording actual additions or subtractions. Hughes found barely one child in 100 voluntarily used the minus sign when asked to record that, say, three bricks had been taken away from a collection of eight. Some tried to show it by drawings, by crossing out the removed items, by arrows, etc. But although they regularly used the subtraction symbol (–) in their written calculations, almost none of them chose to use it in the real situation. This suggests that they did not know what it meant.

The constructivist strategy would be to allow children, initially, to invent whatever recording code they could, and to use their informal notes as a memory aid. These usually carry the meaning well enough, and are often quite as logical as the conventional notation which will be introduced later: for example, 2,2+4 meant '2 and 2 added make 4'. Likewise, db 6,3–3, which is to be read as 'the difference between 6 and 3 makes 3'.

A six-year-old girl (see Gifford 1990) devised a very satisfactory way of showing the operation of subtraction: a curved line, like a hanging chain, linking the numbers whose difference was to be shown (this is compatible with, and perhaps derived from, the number line).

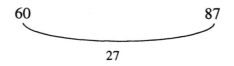

60   87

27

Besides this indulgence in the matter of notation, the constructivist teacher encourages children to use whatever method of computation they feel most comfortable with – while always pressing them to the limits of their methods, and where appropriate offering a better one. Quite often such advances are recognised as short cuts, which improve upon the previous method without invalidating it (there is an important issue of pride here).

Young children often add two sets of objects by firstly counting out each set, then combining them physically, and 'counting all'. This is obviously (to us) unnecessarily laborious, but children may persist with it for months, until one day they realise (or are ready to accept the hint) that, having just counted the larger of the original sets, they are now in a position to 'count on' one integer for every member of the set to be added. This is a highly successful strategy, and not only do some four- and five-year-olds begin to use it, but many people retain it for life.

Subtraction can be done in a similar way, or rather two ways: (a) start with the larger number, then count back one integer for every one of the members of the smaller set; or (b) start with the smaller number, and count on until the larger number is reached. In either case it is necessary to keep count of the number of steps, since this will be the answer; so fingers, or some other spatial aid, may be necessary for keeping this tally. Beginners may find it easier if the intermediate number names are vocalised or sub-vocalised, since it is the number of such names which matters, not their value. Of course, counting on is the perfect method for giving change (money), since the coins or notes themselves take care of this need to keep a record of the difference, which need never be explicitly stated.)

The choice of counting on or counting back will depend upon the closeness of the numbers involved, because it becomes difficult to keep count of more than about 12 steps, and even if this is solved, it is tedious. For larger addenda or differences, some form of idiosyncratic decomposition or redistribution may be used. For example:

(a) 9+22 = 29+2 (count on 2 beyond 29) = 31
(b) 8+15 = 9+14 = 10+13 (use rule for adding 10) = 23

Counting on is rarely taught in schools, since the approved method is to utilise a stock of memorised 'number facts' (or bonds), such as 2+3=5, or 8+9=17. But there are 39 such facts (besides the addition of 1, and including complementaries such as 3+2); so unless the student can recall all of them fluently and confidently, the official method lacks appeal. Lauren Resnick (1983) found that very many six- and seven-year-olds prefer to use counting on, and so do some adults. The artful constructivist would allow the individual to choose – and hopefully thereby avoid the dilemma reported by Sue Atkinson (1992:100):

> Julie (aged 8) sometimes got upset at school because she got her sums wrong. She showed as an example her attempt to add 43 + 8:
>
> $$\begin{array}{r} 43 \\ 8 + \\ \hline 123 \end{array}$$
>
> She got the answer 123, and didn't know whether that was right. But when she was allowed to do the addition by using her fingers (counting on), she got a different result:
> Julie: When you write it, it's 123, but when you do it on your fingers it's 51.
> S.A.: So which is right?
> Julie: 123

S.A.: Why?

Julie: Because you mustn't count on your fingers.

To sum up: the constructivist teacher will not force children to use mathematical methods or notation until they are comfortable with them and know what they are doing. It is harmful to create a gulf between the procedure required by the school and that of common sense, for this can lead to long-term incomprehension and permanent errors. Instead, the teacher will take an interest in the methods which the child chooses to use, and may (when she judges the time to be right) suggest a 'quicker way'. She may also prompt the child to examine cases where the existing method will run into difficulties, as a warning that a better way will have to be found eventually.

When children are engaged on an investigation, the constructivist teacher will respect the child's own efforts, and will try to avoid giving surreptitious assistance. There is always a temptation to help the child to appear to succeed at his/her own attempt, in order to encourage and boost confidence. This is perhaps a patronising attitude, which shields the child from true realisation of the difficulty of the task, and delays the achievement of genuine competence. This means that plenty of time must be allowed, and possibly the chance to return to the problem later. The 'strong constructivist' teacher will not give the answer if the child fails to solve the problem completely, but will give praise for the effort shown and propose a different task.

Practical aids will be available, and children will be encouraged, but not required, to use them. Dienes blocks, the abacus, the calculator; children should be trained in the use of such equipment, but subsequently it should be their decision which to use, and when.

CHAPTER 10

Foundation Subjects and the Whole Curriculum

There is a danger, inherent in any detailed national curriculum, that priority will be given to information and skills, to the detriment of personal development. The constructivist teacher will be aware of the importance of providing ample opportunities for pupils to sort out their own attitudes and values, to review, discuss and revise these, and to refine them through application to a variety of specific cases. Much of this belongs to the 'affective domain' of Bloom's taxonomy – a notoriously neglected part of the curriculum.

Moral education

Let us remember the importance of those two pervasive themes, moral education and personal aesthetics. Attention to these at the lesson planning stage can often give a point to a lesson which would otherwise be dull, and transform it from a routine transmission of information to an experience with personal relevance and significance for the children.

If this is to happen, the lesson must be so designed that children are allowed to participate in a search for personal meaning. This may involve debating an issue, expressing or defending a preference, or interpreting a story: but always in terms of ideas which they are comfortable with. It will help you plan and conduct sessions of this kind if you are familiar with research on conceptual development, particularly in moral education. A useful summary of the stages of progression in 'obedience of rules' (following Piaget (1932) and Kohlberg (1976)) is:

1. Rules are obeyed to avoid punishment.
2. Rules are obeyed to gain social approval.
3. Rules (and laws) are respected if they conform to ethical principles (of equality, justice etc.).

Moral education along these lines is often grounded on real incidents in school life, or in the news, but opportunities can easily be found in stories – either fictional or from history or RE. Willig (1990) reports some research on lying, which found that young children (seven years or less) generally count mistakes and exaggerations as lies, and likely to meet with equally severe punishment (being imprisoned by the police, or burned in hell). Only above eight years did the children consider the *intention* behind the deception, and the possibility of benign ('white') lies.

Kohlberg believes that cognitive conflict is a powerful means of promoting moral development. For example, children aged seven were able to discuss a situation in which a girl had to choose between obeying her parents' strict instructions, and saving a stranded kitten. Many held the opinion that a deed performed with good intentions is a good deed, and should not be punished. Only a few were able to see that the parents' warning, and their fears for the girl's safety, also needed to be considered.

Teachers who were introduced to the theory of stages in moral development, and who were shown how to use 'cognitive conflict' materials such as the kitten story, accepted that the children's moral decisions could only be as well-founded as each child's understanding would allow. This is in contrast with traditionally-minded teachers who felt duty-bound to inform the children of their own correct judgements, which they expected the children to accept (Willig 1990:178).

I feel that one of the statements of 'Desirable outcomes on entry to compulsory schooling' (SCAA 1996:9) could well be applied right through the primary school, if approached through the eliciting and encouraging of children's own judgements:

> Children are sensitive to the needs and feelings of others, and show respect for people of other cultures and beliefs. They take turns and share fairly. They express their feelings and behave in appropriate ways, developing an understanding of what is right, what is wrong *and why*. They treat living things, property and the environment with care and concern. They respond to relevant cultural and religious events and show a range of feelings, such as wonder, joy or sorrow, in response to their experiences of the world. (My italics.)

Dave Francis (1996) makes some suggestions for classroom activities of this type. Let the children gaze at a computer-generated stereograph (such as a 3-D tetrahedral star), and then talk about the idea that 'there's more to life than meets the eye'. Discuss the question, 'Are all disasters avoidable, if people took proper precautions? Or are some disasters unavoidable? If so, is anyone to blame?' 'Is bad luck sent by God, or spirits, as punishment for bad behaviour?'

We can invent questions like this to suit the abilities of the class. 'Have you ever been afraid of something, and then found that you had made a mistake? How do you feel about it now?' 'What is a mystery? Give an example. Can you always expect to solve a mystery – that is, to find the answer – by careful investigation? Or are there some that will never be answered?'

It is important to plan for moral education instruction, and not leave it to spontaneous development of current issues. Advantages of planning are: you can decide in advance which moral principles to include and which to avoid; which cases to use to raise or exemplify these issues; the language demands of your questions or materials; and the possibility of causing anxiety for certain individuals (perhaps because of their religion).

Religious education might seem to be closely related to moral education, but this is not necessarily the case (it could take the form of instruction, for instance, or historical information). However, most religious stories carry an implicit moral message, and it will usually make for a more interesting lesson if these are brought out for discussion, rather than treated as given. Stories of the saints, martyrs or prophets are often intended to illustrate moral virtues such as bravery, unshakeable faith, national pride, or opposition to corruption or oppression. In such cases the children may be invited to take the story apart, to recognise these moral virtues, and to say how they might apply today (under different circumstances). By such means the pupils may be helped to construct interpretations which are meaningful for themselves. Christian, Hindu, Buddhist and many other parables offer opportunities for thoughtful, philosophical reflection and sharing.

Geography education

Geography education, too, could be made more personally relevant through the inclusion of ethical and aesthetic considerations. Children are often given the task of drawing a map of their local area, but if this is handled insensitively it can fail to record or communicate the child's knowledge. The child's mental map will be idiosyncratic, and not at all like the published maps; it may emphasise interesting features and reduce or omit boring parts. In response to a request to 'imagine your journey from home to school, and then draw a map of it', one child drew only the interior of the car she was carried to school in. Another drew almost no streets except for the bridge over the river, which was shown in flamboyant detail, with boats below. Further research revealed that children aged eight often drew a different map for the homeward journey, even though it was along the same route as had been taken in the morning.

Other 'maps', when accompanied by a verbal account, showed that the noise, crowds, and smell of the journey were more significant than the plain geography: we should not overlook this. Likewise, if a child's impression of a foreign country is limited to the holiday beach, it is none the less authentic. We should aim to augment, not replace, those personal experiences.

An ethical issue arises as soon as we begin to study the ways of life of foreign populations. Children are quite likely to have picked up impressions of developing countries as having picturesque ways (camels, thatched huts, women washing clothes in the river, etc.), and assume that the people live in these ways entirely by choice. A well-planned geography lesson will not only convey information (which, in any case, is no longer a compulsory part of the National Curriculum), but could open up questions of how culture is related to necessity, and how traditional values can be at odds with economics. A similar theme for discussion is the meaning and status of the 'foreigner'. Some young children were asked, after some conversation about foreigners, whether they themselves would become foreigners if they were to go abroad; and the majority denied any such possibility. Nationality, ethnicity, social class, equal opportunities – these are all aspects of geography which have powerful ethical and personal meaning, and may well need to take priority over topography or climate studies (yes – even pollution and acid rain seem too remote from the child's experience to be suitable topics unless set in a specific context). Of course the teacher will be careful not to introduce too much too soon, and the story approach, or a discussion of pictures or a video clip, will often be the method used. A teachers' handbook with many suggestions of this kind is Values and Visions (Burns and Lamont 1995). 'Alemitu's story' and 'What did they do?' in this book both relate to the need for clean water; 'The banks of a river' is a problem-situation activity about pollution. Oxfam's education department is another source of materials for ethical geography studies.

If economic awareness (the world of work) is on the agenda, the constructivist approach could be invaluable, helping to show the children's range of understanding of the concepts required. For example, Willig (1990:128) reports some research into six- and seven-year-olds' notions of shops and trade: the young ones considered the exchange of goods for money as a kind of game, and thought it likely that the money received would be given back, or given to charity. Some older children knew that the shopkeeper would have to pay money for more goods, to replace those sold, but assumed that the price would be the same as the retail price – i.e. a non-profit business. How the assistants could be paid without selling off stock was a mystery. Some children think that money is obtainable (free of charge!) from the slot in the wall: which is only an update on their well-known belief that milk is manufactured at the supermarket. I mention these facts just to make the point that these children could easily have been totally confused by a transmission lesson on shops which took for granted even a rudimentary grasp of commerce.

The ethical approach to geography education deserves further attention. If we keep our teaching in touch with questions of beliefs and values, we not only enhance motivation, but we increase the probability of successful communication of ideas. If any of our pupils find our ideas and meanings unclear, they will generally disregard them; but if they feel that they matter, then they are that much more likely to persevere, and to challenge us to explicate more fully; and if we invite them to respond with suggestions of their own, we will be able to assess, instantly, whether we are beginning to share meanings. And that must be a good basis for education, whatever the subject.

Part III
A Philosophical Overview

CHAPTER 11
Probing Deeper

Constructivism as a pedagogic theory

This book began with an attempt, in Chapter 1, to define the constructivist approach, at least up to the point from which it could be distinguished from other methods. I showed that it must not be confused with the discovery method (or 'enquiry method'), although both share the characteristic of pupil participation. Nor is it a self-teaching method, although the learner does share with the teacher the responsibility for what is learned.

The most widely used alternative to constructivist teaching is undoubtedly the transmission method. I feel that we should now take a closer look at the theoretical bases of these two, and to attempt to appraise them.

Throughout the book there has been an implied assumption that the constructivist approach is a good, or even the best, teaching method. Can this theory be supported by evidence, or put to the test? Has there been any empirical research into the effectiveness of this method in comparison with another? Or is it just a matter of taste ... a method loved by some teachers and hated by others?

Does the approach have 'objective' characteristics which transcend the effects of an individual teacher's personality and skill? Or is the appraisal, like many a political or religious argument, so tied up with values, cultural traditions, and historical loyalties that a balanced judgement is impossible to reach?

The answer to all these questions is, of course 'yes and no'. But that need not stop us from trying to sort out what part of the claims we would support, and what we would be very cautious about. The goal, which is better education for children (and indeed all students), is too important to allow us to give up the search just because it is going to get complicated.

At this point I believe we need some fuller definitions, and I propose that you study the following table, noting similarities and differences.

Constructivist	Transmissionist
1. Constructivist teaching has, as a central long-term aim, the encouragement of the pupil's mental capabilities: intellectual, aesthetic and ethical, as well as encouraging ingenuity, creativity and fluency in the application of knowledge to novel situations.	1. Transmissionist teaching has, as a central long-term aim, the encouragement of the pupil's mental capabilities: predominantly intellectual but with some regard for the aesthetic, spiritual and moral, and the gaining of secure knowledge (both practical and theoretical) and the ability to apply it to a known range of situations.
2. A constructivist teaching approach must be built on a constructivist theory of learning: briefly, that the learner always controls what sense he/she makes of any experience or instruction (including the words and pictures offered by the teacher, books, videos or computer programmes). In the last resort, the learning that takes place is completely restricted to what the student chooses to learn.	2. A transmissionist teaching approach holds the teacher (and curriculum) mainly responsible for the effectiveness and extent of the learning. Information should be presented to the pupil in a clear, systematic yet stimulating way, so that learning becomes a pleasure. Resistance to learning (e.g. boredom, disinterest[1], confusion, or lack of prerequisite knowledge) must be recognised and overcome by the teacher's skill, energy, resourcefulness and strength of character. 'You never forget a good teacher', as they say.
3. Successful teaching will lead to growth of understanding, breadth of vision, a wish to pursue enquiry, and a more mature, fluent and articulate style of conversation. The pupil's stock of knowledge, at any given moment, will be idiosyncratic (i.e. patchy) but capable of being expanded rapidly when any particular need arises.	3. Successful teaching will lead to growth of the pupil's stock of knowledge and understanding, an improvement in the accuracy and scope of these ideas, and an increased facility (both in speed and accuracy) in the performance of academic exercises. Well educated students will hold more or less the same stock of knowledge, which allows assessment to be reliable.
	1 In the new sense of hostile attitude to a topic.

To return to the opening question(s): what research has been or could be done to test the claim that the constructivist method is superior (or vice versa)? A classical 'teaching experiment' in the scientific paradigm would require matched populations of children, each pre-tested to ensure initial identity of scholastic performance in some selected area; each group would then be taught, for equal times, by equally competent teachers, but in accordance with the different pedagogical methodologies. Then tests of attainment would be administered, and the scores compared statistically, to determine whether there was a significant difference.

I think it is fair to say that such an approach to research in social science has now been totally discredited, and no such 'experiment' would ever be attempted. The main objection concerns the validity of the test instruments: the attainment test would be likely to favour the transmission group, because their teaching aims are closer to the kind of attainment that can most easily be assessed through group tests or examinations (knowledge of facts, routine application of principles, prescribed skills etc.). It might on the other hand be possible to devise a test of the attainments aimed for by the constructivist teachers (some areas of deep knowledge, persistence in enquiry, etc.), but not only would this be invalid for the comparison group, it would not even be reliable for the constructivist group, because the approximate nature of the scores would make it impossible to be sure that the final ability was definitely an improvement on that measured in the pre-test.

If we accept the impossibility of measuring the kind of educational outcome that constructivist teaching aims for, we might fall back on long-term classroom assessment for the evidence. Surely if the teacher is doing something right it will make an observable difference. At its simplest we could apply the pragmatic criterion, that is, that the method works.

But who is to do the observing? The teacher herself, as in Action Research? A colleague or coordinator? An independent (!) academic researcher? Or an Inspector of Schools? And what specific criteria should be used? Pupil behaviour (e.g. time-on-task, or apparent enjoyment) might be measured, but the scores would be impossible to interpret. Does a quiet, docile class count as a success or a failure, constructivistly speaking? And even in the area of knowledge acquisition the outcome might be difficult to compare, for if we take seriously the constructivists' claim that *lasting* learning can only be acquired through the pupil's willing participation, we shall have to ignore those tests at the end of term (or Key Stage), and come back in ten years time.

This would, of course, be moving the goal posts. But the attempt to measure the relative merits of the two teaching approaches begins to resemble a sporting contest with goals that are not only moving, but of indefinite size, and shrouded in mist. So let us abandon any attempt to 'prove' the claims of the two teaching methods, and enter instead into a philosophical debate about values.

Mary Hesse (1978:12–13) held that:

> The criteria for acceptability [of theories in social science] are *pluralist* – as pluralist as our choices of value goals. And if we wish to talk of values it also follows that we presuppose a certain area of freedom in the activity of theorising – we are not wholly constrained to adopt particular theories either by the facts ... or by social and economic environment.

So, insofar as pedagogy is a social science, we may construct any theory that seems likely, and without any obligation to submit to 'evidence' (since it can never be conclusive), nor to accept the current ideology (such as 'market forces'). The reason why no measured results can ever be taken as conclusive is the multitude of variable conditions. The ardent constructivist teacher can usually discount (explain away) any setbacks by claiming adverse conditions (over-large class size, parental preoccupation with 'traditional' progress markers). Perhaps the obstacles to improvement will be institutional, and virtually impossible to remove; that would be a defeatist theory. But there may still be ways for individual advance, through honest philosophical reflection, through informed, on-the-spot mentoring, and through reading.

Insofar as pedagogy is an art, success is attained only when the teacher is personally convinced that what she has done is right for the children. That is evidence, of a kind.

Confusion and frustration: possible outcomes of a constructivist strategy?

Philosophical (linguistic) analysis can sometime be useful to teachers. For example, let's consider a fairly common anxiety that children can become 'confused' by oblique teaching. It is not unusual for them to complain that they have been 'confused' by some episode of constructivist teaching. The symptoms are that the child now, after the lesson, feels that he does not understand something. Perhaps we can unpack this situation, so as to be in a better position to know what to do about it. I believe we should consider two entirely distinct states of mind, which I call (1) epistemological confusion and (2) social confusion.

Type 1 arises when a person thought that they knew or understood something, but, through the teacher's questions and suggestions, is led to realise that they aren't sure. The old certainty has been shaken, but the glimpse of the better model (explanation) is still unclear and out of reach. Because it is the state of their knowledge that is in question, this is epistemological confusion; and it may be only temporary. It may be an essential intermediate state (as in a chrysalis), while the learner re-evaluates preconceptions, and constructs new ideas.

Someone said that a good story should have 'a beginning, a muddle and an end'. If all goes well, concept development is like that: recognition of imperfect understanding, and a struggle to sort things out, culminating in a new, stable and (at least temporarily) satisfactory model. Remember, though, that clumsy teaching can lead to unnecessary and unpleasant cognitive loss. A teacher can inadvertently destroy a child's existing understanding (by rubbishing it), without succeeding in replacing it by anything else.

The other sort of 'confusion', which I have labelled 'social' (type 2), may be less serious but probably more common. It is a pupil's misunderstanding of the 'rules of engagement' which the constructivist teacher is trying to establish.

Consider a pupil who has come (from past experience) to expect that the teacher will convey knowledge, which the pupils have to learn and reproduce on demand. Under these rules, to 'play fair' the teacher must make it very clear what has to be learned. It is, according to these same transmissionist rules, unfair for a teacher to question or test a child on something that has not been taught. 'But Miss! We haven't done that yet, Miss.' Objection sustained.

This pupil now comes into the care of a teacher who uses a constructivist strategy, and thereby violates either or both of these rules. This leaves the pupil 'confused' as to what answer will be acceptable; and since (under the previous regime) failure to answer correctly often led to disgrace and even punishment, this social predicament is very uncomfortable. The teacher may say, over and over again, 'It doesn't matter if you're wrong', but the child, conditioned to the old rules, just won't believe it.

Children aren't stupid. It may be that the teacher is fooling her/himself, and is actually sending mixed messages: constructivist open-ended intentions but closed, 'right-answer' practices. Many a class discussion starts with, 'Has anyone any ideas?' but closes with a teacher-approved version which must be accepted by all. I suggest that if you want an unambiguously radical constructivist class session, you must be explicit in planning and establishing the lesson, and consistent in your own role. Make it clear what sort of lesson it is going to be. It is very difficult to achieve transmission of information and at the same time to require pupils to investigate or try out their own ideas; so if you have knowledge-transfer objectives, don't pretend that it is brainstorm time. It is no disgrace to say, 'No, I'm not inviting your ideas this lesson, because I want you to listen to *my* ideas'. Even a convinced constructivist will frequently need to teach information (or conventional behaviours) 'as given' and not 'as constructed': e.g. days of the week, spelling rules, or just the instructions for the class trip. Remember, though, that pupils will often distort, misinterpret or mis-hear this supposedly objective information.

In your anxiety to get your pupils to accept your new constructivist regime, you may find yourself telling them, 'it's all right: there are no wrong answers'. This is, taken literally, misleading. What you mean is to assure them that you don't already have one single right answer in mind, so there are quite a number of possible answers. But there may be answers that you will decide to challenge, either because (1) they are 'off target' and don't correspond to the question, or (2) they are logically inconsistent with the given assumptions, or (3) they are contradicted by observable facts known to the pupils (some examples were given in Chapter 3). So it is not the case (as opponents have claimed) that in the constructivist approach, 'anything goes'. In fact a lot of difficulty has come about because the term 'constructivism' has been used in so many different ways (Bell and Gilbert 1996:44ff). It is this confusion (that word again!) that I shall now try to sort out.

Different versions of constructivism

Pedagogic constructivism is a theory of teaching which presents an alternative – a 'middle way' – between transmission (exposition/reception)

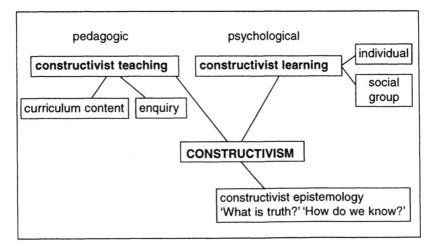

Figure 9 A concept analysis for constructivism.

teaching and the discovery method. This was the point with which this book began. In the extreme form, transmission teaching assumes that the teacher has knowledge and the pupil has none (or none that can be useful); and so the empty mind is filled, as if by pouring knowledge in from a jug. In complete contrast, the 'discovery' teacher regards the child's mind as something which will grow to fruition; the teacher's job is to tend it, by encouragement and provision of stimulating opportunities. I have tried to suggest that both of these traditional methods may have their part to play in a balanced curriculum: there will be times for learning facts, and times for educative play. But there will also be an important role for the systematic, professional mediation between learner and cognitive development, in which teacher and learner share the responsibility for learning. This is pedagogic constructivism.

The theory of teaching must be based upon a theory of learning, and this is where some differences arise (there is a concise and useful view of such research in 'What we know about Effective Primary Teaching' by Caroline Gipps (1992)). Psychologists have studied learning under controlled, scientific conditions, but most of the early work in experimental psychology is useless as a guide for constructivist pedagogy, because it was concerned with memory and recall of small units of knowledge (for example, isolated words or strings of digits) rather than the acquisition of meaningful concepts. Jean Piaget was the first influential writer in the field of meaningful learning, and his theory, which he called 'genetic epistemology', may perhaps be described as positing the construction of knowledge through individual mental growth, as a consequence of individual interaction with experience. Constructivist pedagogy of the 1970s and 80s continued to hold Piaget's view of intellectual growth as an individual affair, although the emphasis on across-the-board mental abilities (the concrete and formal 'operations') was replaced by progression of context-specific concepts (Figure 4's ladders). Learning is assumed to occur through either (i) the routine 'assimilation' of new information into existing schemes/models, or (ii) the 'accommodation' of new information and experience by means of restructuring or even replacing those schemes/models. Sometimes new ideas can be invented by the learner, but probably more often they will be received from the intellectual environment, and modified according to personal need. This theory of learning centres on the individual learner's efforts. Knowledge grows because it is *made* – made out of bits and pieces, like a shanty-town house, or a bower bird's display.

An exciting development in cognitive science may show why this is so. Gerald Edelman's (1992) theory of neuronal group selection describes the formation of concepts as the retention and strengthening of neural paths in the brain which initially occur by chance, but are reinforced by repeated use (paths which are never used again simply atrophy and die). The only principle, besides experience, which guides the selection of pathways is that the resultant thoughts must be of *value* to the person, and by this is meant instinctive value such as survival, sex, or the satisfaction of hunger.

> Because of its linkage to value and to the concept of self, this system of meaning is almost never free of affect; it is charged with emotions.
>
> (Edelman 1992:170)

I think that this has implications for learning and for motivation. In order for a new idea to be assimilated, it must be recognised as being of value; and our organ for this recognition may be the 'primitive' limbic system. I do not mean that every new idea which is retained has to be of immediate utility, but it must satisfy some general drive such as curiosity, beauty, parent-child bonding. Who knows, exactly? (We must resist the temptation to speculate beyond the evidence, as the sociobiologists have been accused of doing.)

Recently a new view of constructivist learning has become popular, in which knowledge was constructed not by the isolated learner but by the social group. Under the influence of Lev Vygotsky, a new theory of socially constructed meaning emerged. Accordingly, children learn through two-way communication of ideas with other people: other children (peers), parents, and of course, teachers. They see people behaving in certain ways, appropriate to the situation, and so they try to copy them, and this includes speech. Children try out ideas for size, through conversation. Learning is, at least in part, driven by the desire to communicate. Cognition is itself a social construct (see Berger and Luckmann (1966); Resnick *et al.* (1991)). The message for constructivist teachers is clear: let the children talk!

Besides the shift from individual to social constructivism, another dichotomy or split has occurred. Most writers (including myself!) took it for granted that the learner would only proceed to build/adopt a difficult or complicated model if his or her earlier, simpler one was found, personally, to be unsatisfactory. Then the learner would abandon the old model and adopt the new, in a way that resembles Thomas Kuhn's 1962 account of scientific revolution through 'paradigm shift'. One of the key papers setting out this 'displacement' model for conceptual change was by Posner *et al.* (1982), but it is found in most books of the period (1970–1990) concerned with science education. Recently a different model has been proposed (see Gunstone 1995:66): the learner's previous ideas are not necessarily rejected when they are found wanting, but are retained for use *when possible*. The more difficult, newly-acquired ideas are brought into use only when it is known that the easier ones will fail. This view of progression as pluralistic accretion is implicit in my own (Selley 1996d) treatment of phenomenography and the 'Towers of San Gimignano' metaphor. As an illustration of this type of phenomenography, consider the progression of models for air, from around five years of age.

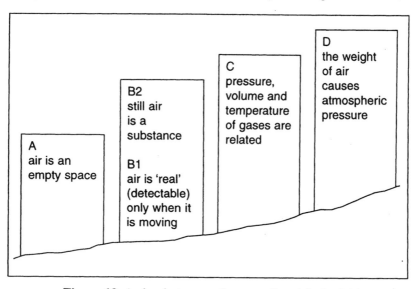

Figure 10 A simple towers diagram of models for 'air'.

As we mature (cognitively) we adopt successive models, and most adults are probably familiar with at least model C. But even model A ('Air is empty space') is not totally rejected: think of an 'empty' milk bottle, or the common (but dangerous) assumption that exhaust fumes from a car 'just disappear into the air'.

To sum up: the constructivist view of knowledge is a pluralistic one: very little is absolutely right or wrong, and most is a matter of judgement. Even in science there are alternative models which are incomplete or limited in scope, but which are useful in some contexts, and it is up to us to choose (on pedagogical grounds) when to accept or even propose one as the basis for explanation and prediction, or when to try to teach the next step up.

Postscript to Chapter 11: A chat about ontology

What is real? We have good reason to doubt that we can observe the world perfectly accurately. So, 'What is the real world?'

Nobody knows for sure.

But you would claim that the experts, using the latest scientific equipment, have *nearly* got it right?

Well, no, I wouldn't say that. Sometimes new theories come along, which completely change our descriptions. A century ago no-one knew anything about vitamins, or hormones ... nor, of course, about deficiency diseases.

So perhaps we should accept that the ultimate real world will never be known?

That's it. All we can do is experiment and observe and calculate the best theoretical description we can think of.

A model?

Yes – construct our best model, and use it for practical purposes, and for research ...

Until, I suppose, someone thinks up a better one. So, if we had been born in a different century, say 5,000 years earlier or later than now, we would see almost everything as different?

I'd go along with that.

So why do we accept that what we all think now is *right*, when obviously it must be *wrong*?

It's not so much wrong as – er – different.

So according to you, nothing can be a wrong idea? If I wanted to, I could say that my beer glass is still full, even though I've drunk it all!

No, no. Even the most modern (or postmodern) philosophers don't go *that* far. Your claim would have to be backed up by evidence, and withstand all logical and experimental tests.

So that's settled then. My glass *is* empty, even to a critical realist like you?

Yes.

Well then, what are you waiting for?

References

Appleby, J., Hunt, L. Jacob, M. (1994) 'Telling the truth about history', *see* Murphy (1996).

Aris, M. (1993) 'History teaching in the primary school', in Brooks, R., Aris, M., Perry, I. (1993) *The Effective Teaching of History*. Harlow: Longman.

Atkinson, S. (ed.) (1992) *Mathematics with Reason*. London: Hodder and Stoughton Educational.

Baker, K. (1991) *The Turbulent Years*. London: Faber.

Barnes, D. (1992) 'The role of talk in learning', in Norman, K. (ed.) *Thinking Voices: the work of the National Oracy Project*. London: Hodder and Stoughton Educational.

Barnes, D. (1976) *From Communication to Curriculum*. London: Penguin.

Barnes, D., Britton, J., Rosen, H. (1971) *Language, Learner and the School*, 3rd edn. London: Penguin.

Bell, B. and Gilbert, J. (1996) *Teacher Development: A Model from Science Education*. London: Falmer.

Berger, P. and Luckmann, T. (1966) *The Social Construction of Reality: A Treatise in the Sociology of Knowledge*. London: Penguin.

Burns, S. and Lamont, G. (1995) *Values and Visions: A Handbook for Spiritual Development and Global Awareness*. London: Hodder and Stoughton Educational.

Carey, S. (1985) *Conceptual Change in Childhood*. Mass./London: MIT Press.

Comber, M. and Johnson, P. (1995) 'Pushes and pulls: the potential of concept mapping for assessment', *Primary Science Review* **36**, 10–12.

Davis, A. and Pettit, D. (eds) (1994) *Developing Understanding in Primary Mathematics*. London: Falmer.

Department for Education and Science (DES) (1989) National Curriculum for England and Wales: Science.

DfEE (1998a) *Teaching: High Status, High Standards*. London: Department for Education and Employment.

DfEE (1998b) *The National Literacy Strategy. Framework for Teaching*. London: Department for Education and Employment.

Driver, R. *et al.* (1985) *Children's Ideas in Science*. Buckingham: Open University Press.

Drummond, M. J. (1993) *Assessing Children's Learning*. London: David Fulton Publishers.

Edelman, G. (1992) *Bright Air, Brilliant Fire: On the Matter of the Mind*. London: Penguin.

Egan, K. (1988) *Primary Understanding*. London: Routledge.

Eisner, E. W. (1982) *Cognition and Curriculum*. New York: Longman.

Francis, D. (1996) *Just a Thought: exploring religious ideas*. London: Hodder and Stoughton.

Gipps, C. (1992) *What we know about Effective Primary Teaching*. London: Tufnell Press.

Glasersfeld, E. von (1995) *Radical Constructivism*. London: Falmer.

Gunstone, R. (1995) 'Can we prepare teachers to teach the way students learn?' in Hofstein, A. *et al.* (eds) *Science Education: From Theory to Practice*. Israel: Weizmann Institute of Science.

Hall, N. (ed.) (1989) *Writing with Reason: the Emergence of Authorship in Young Children*. London: Hodder and Stoughton Educational.

Hesse, M. (1978) 'Theory and values in the social sciences', in Hookway, C. and Pettit, P. (eds) *Action and Interpretation*. Cambridge: Cambridge University Press.

Hughes, M. (1986) *Children and Number*. Oxford: Blackwell.

Keogh, B. and Naylor, S. (1997) *Starting Points for Science*. Oxford: Millgate House.

Kohlberg, L. (1976) 'Moral stages and moralization: the cognitive developmental approach', in Likona, T. (ed) *Moral Development and Behaviour*. London: Holt Rinehart and Winston.

Labinowicz, (ed.) (1985) *Learning from Children: new beginnings for teaching numerical thinking (a Piagetian approach)*. Reading, Mass.: Addison-Wesley.

Lee, P. *et al.* (1995) 'Progression in children's ideas about history', in Hughes, M. (ed.) (1995) *Progression in Learning*. BERA Dialogues: Multilingual Matters.

Lee, P. *et al.* (1996) 'Concepts of history and teaching approaches at Key Stages 2 and 3', *Teaching History* 82, 6–11.

Light, P. *et al.* (eds) (1991) *Learning to Think*. Oxford: Oxford University Press.

Littledyke, M. and Huxford, L. (eds) (1998) *Teaching the Primary Curriculum for Constructive Learning*. London: David Fulton Publishers.

Matthews, M. R. (1994) *Science Teaching: the role of History and Philosophy of Science*. London: Routledge

Millar, R. and Lubben, F. (March 1996) 'Investigative work in science: the role of prior expectations and evidence in shaping conclusions', *Education 3 to 13*.

Mills, C. and Timson, L. (1988) *Looking at Language in the Primary School*. Sheffield: National Association for the Teaching of English.

Murphy, S. (October 1996) 'A practical realist take on post-modernism', *Teaching History* 85, 4–5.

O'Hear, P. and White, J. (1993) *Assessing the National Curriculum*. London: Paul Chapman Publishing.

Osborne, J. *et al.* (1990) *Primary SPACE Report: Light*. Liverpool: Liverpool University Press.

Piaget, J. (1930) *The Child's Conception of Physical Causality*. London: Routledge & Kegan Paul.

Piaget, J. (1932) *The Moral Judgement of the Child*. Routledge & Kegan Paul.

Posner, G. J. *et al.* (1982) 'Accommodation of a scientific conception: Towards a theory of conceptual change', *Science Education* **66**, 211–227.

Resnick, L. (1982) in Ginsburg, H. (ed.) *The Development of Mathematical Thinking*. London: Academic Press.

Resnick, L. *et al.* (1991) *Perspectives on Socially Shared Cognition*. Washington, American Psychological Association.

Robson, S. and Smedley, S. (1996) *Education in Early Childhood*. London: David Fulton Publishers.

Russell, T. and Watt, D. (1990) *Evaporation and Condensation*. Liverpool: Liverpool University Press.

Sainsbury, M. (1996) *Tracking Significant Achievement in Primary English*. London: Hodder and Stoughton Educational.

SCAA (Schools Curriculum and Assessment Authority) (1995a) *Planning the Curriculum at Key Stages 1 and 2*. London: SCAA.

SCAA (1995b) *Report of the KS2 Tests in English, Mathematics and Science*. London: SCAA.

SCAA (1996) *Desirable Outcomes on Entry to Compulsory Schooling*. London: SCAA.

SEAC (Schools Examinations and Assessment Council) (n.d. 1990) *A Guide to Teacher Assessment*, Pack C, 38.

Selley, N. J. (1998) 'The plague of the 'right-word' assessment', *Primary Science Review* **53**, 31–32.

Selley, N. J. (1996) *Children's Ideas about Earth and Sky*. Kingston University, Faculty of Business.

Selley, N. J. (1995) *An Investigation into Children's Ideas on Light and Vision*. Kingston University, Faculty of Business.

Selley, N. J. (1993) 'Why do things float? A study of the place for alternative models in school science', *School Science Review* **74**, 55–61.

Shapiro, B. (1994) *What Children Bring to Light*. New York: Teachers College Press.

Smith, L. and Holden, C. (June 1994) 'I thought it was for picking bones out of soup … using artefacts in the primary school', *Teaching History* **76**, 6–9.

Solomon, J. (1980) *Teaching Children in the Laboratory*. London: Croom Helm.

Tizard, B. and Hughes, M. (1984) *Young Children Learning*. London: Fontana.

Wadsworth, P. (1997) 'When do I tell them the right answer?', *Primary Science Review* **49**, 23–4.

Willig, C. J. (1990) *Children's Concepts and the Primary Curriculum*. London: Paul Chapman Publishing.

Index

Lightning Source UK Ltd.
Milton Keynes UK
UKOW03f0923240117

292742UK00001B/2/P